THE WORD OF THE LORD

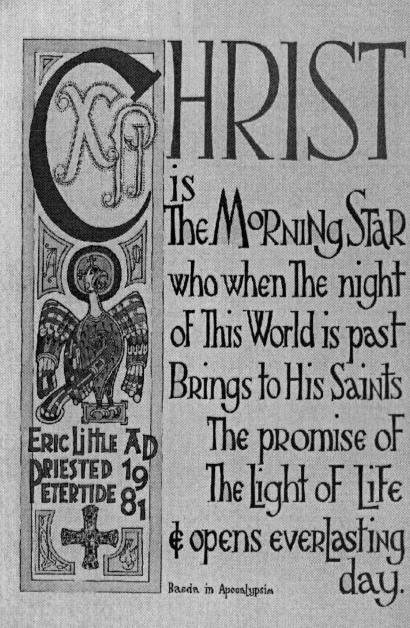

CHRIST
is
The Morning Star
who when The night
of This World is past
Brings to His Saints
The promise of
The Light of Life
& opens everlasting
day.

Eric Little AD
Priested 19
Petertide 81

Baeda in Apocalypsim

ii

THE WORD OF THE LORD

A Short Guidebook to all the Books of the Old and New Testaments

The Reverend H. E. S. (Eric) Little

Visit us online at www.authorsonline.co.uk

An AuthorsOnLine Book

ISBN 0 7552 0183 3

Authors OnLine Ltd
40 Castle Street
Hertford SG14 1HR
England

This book is also available in e-book format, details of which are available at
www.authorsonline.co.uk

Dedicated to my dear wife, Emily

SELECTIONS FROM THE OLD AND NEW TESTAMENTS

WE PREACH CHRIST:-

About The Author

The Reverend H.E.S.Little, ("Eric"), was born in Bath, England, and educated at South Twerton Junior School and The Crypt School Gloucester, winning a scholarship to read Classics at Exeter College, Oxford. However, national service during World War II intervened and he later gained his degrees of B.A. and B.D. through the extra mural department of the University of London. After teaching Religious Education in schools for many years in Gloucester he lectured in Religious Education at Neville's Cross Teachers Training College, Durham, (now part of New College, University of Durham). Having been a lay-reader for many years in the Church of England, Eric was ordained priest in 1981 in Durham Cathedral.

Eric's profound wish is that this book will help readers to explore the Bible and discover the eternal truth of God's love for each one of us.

General Introduction

During the years that I have studied, taught and lectured on the Bible, my love of Holy Scripture has steadily increased. In this condensed version of the Bible I now wish to present some of the passages from the Old and New Testaments which have proved invaluable and a source of inspiration to me and to those whom I have taught.

I am not assuming that the Bible may be read without help; for I myself, as all readers of the Bible (see Acts 8.vv.30-31) owe an incalculable debt to those who have expounded the Scriptures in teaching, preaching, writing Commentaries and Bible Reading notes. I believe, however, that the most effective and valuable way of studying the "Book of Books" is first to be guided into reading such passages as have here been selected, allowing these passages to "speak for themselves", and in "We Preach Christ" sharing Gospel insights.

It has been remarked that the Bible is "not a book that I read, but one that reads me". I am convinced that this is true; for it is a book that challenges and disturbs. As "Mark Twain" (Samuel Clements) once remarked, "Other people are worried about the Biblical passages they can't understand; as for me it is the passages that I do understand that worry me!".

It is my sincere hope that this book may bring some of its readers to a greater love for the "Word of the Lord".

H. E. S. Little, B.D., B.A

HOW TO READ THE WORD OF THE LORD

Every book of the Old and New Testament is represented in this study and references are given to the 'recommended passages.' Any version of the Bible may be used, but it is suggested that for the sake of clarity and modern scholarship the 'New Revised Standard Version' be used.

FOREWARD TO THE OLD TESTAMENT

This Bible Guidebook is written from a Christian viewpoint and based upon Christian insights; but since Jesus Christ was a Jew for whom the Old Testament was his Bible, we need to highlight those themes that we are seeking to illustrate in our selection of Old Testament passages:-

The Old Testament is a written record of God searching out mankind, and mankind's response to God's call. As St. Augustine said, "I would not even have sought you, O Lord, if you had not first found me". Throughout the whole of the Old Testament runs the theme of God in his loving kindness reaching out to mankind.

God is revealed as Creator and Sovereign Lord of all that is. His Creation is good and his purposes for mankind benevolent.

God is represented not only as a loving Father, but one whose judgements stand fast. "God is not mocked", as St. Paul declared (Galatians 6.v.7), and to attempt to thwart the declared will of God entails spiritual death.

The Prophets, or "spokesmen for God" declare God's purposes for his people, giving them warning and encouragement.

Particularly in the Psalter (and elsewhere) we have passages of great beauty that bring strength and comfort to God's people, passages that are dearly beloved by Jew and Christian alike.

The Old Testament is a record of the history of a remarkable people bound together with their God in a Covenant relationship and prepared, as Christians maintain, for the Advent of the "Word made Flesh", the Incarnate Son of God.

INDEX TO CONTENTS OF THE OLD TESTAMENT

INDEX TO CONTENTS OF THE OLD TESTAMENT
(continued)

Old Testament Passages

GENESIS

The book Genesis, as its title suggests, deals with the 'beginnings' - the Creation, the early history of Israel and mankind's approach and response to a loving God who first finds mankind and reveals His name and nature.

Some of the most beautiful and profound passages in the Bible are contained in this book. The myths, legends and history contained in it are deservedly as popular today as they ever were.

Genesis 1 to 4 v.16

The story of the Tower of Babel has interesting and valuable insights particularly in reference to the Christian observance of the Feast of Pentecost.

Genesis 11.vv.1-9

The full account of the early days of Abram are lost in the mists of time but the account of his call and departure from Haran shows the importance of Abram as the 'Father of the Nation of Israel'. God's gracious promises to His people are enshrined in a 'Covenant' to which generations of Jews have looked back and which they hold is still binding.

Genesis 12.vv.1-9

The gripping story of the near-sacrifice of Isaac is for many Christian people linked with the account of the Cross of Christ.

Genesis 22.vv1-19

We include the charming story of Isaac (Abram's son) and Rebekah but omit the further details of Abram's descendants.

Genesis .24.vv.1-67

The stories of deception by Jacob his son and by Rebekah his wife upon Isaac, the cheating of Esau by Jacob and their outcome are omitted, but taken up in the account of Jacob fleeing his brother's wrath and finding God still with him in exile and disgrace.

Genesis 27.vv.21-45, and 28.vv.10-22

The account of 'Wrestling Jacob', the happy reunion with Esau and the changing of Jacob's name to 'Israel' is of the utmost importance.

Genesis 32.vv.9-31

The promise of God to Jacob/Israel and the reference to Bethel are of great importance in understanding the history and religion of the nation.

Genesis 35.vv.9-15

Even if the historical details of Israel's stay in Egypt could be established, very little of importance and interest would be gained by their inclusion, but the story of Joseph in Egypt is splendidly told. It contains a fascinating account of God's dealing with Jacob's son who on first acquaintance is far from being a loveable character until God 'takes him in hand'. A brief passage forms a link with the book Exodus.

Genesis 50.vv.24-26

EXODUS

The passages selected from this book are chosen to illustrate the theme that God rescued His people from slavery in Egypt. This conviction of Israel is at the very heart of the 'Good News' and for Christians looks forward to that immeasurably greater event when God sent His Son to be the Saviour of the world.

The exact historical details of the Exodus are not verifiable and are doubtless intermixed with saga, legends and myths, but the call of Moses as 'Servant of the Lord' and the outline of the Exodus events speak of an act of God which is historically based and of supreme religious importance.

Exodus 3.vv.1-17

The narrative of Passover is so important in the Old and the New Testaments that a brief account of it is essential. Doubtless it is based upon a genuine remembrance of a series of catastrophes that struck the Egyptians, facilitating the escape of the people of Israel and in which they perceived the hand of God.

Exodus 12.vv.1-13

The crossing of the 'Sea of Reeds' (Yam Suph, the 'Red Sea') enabled the Israelites to escape the pursuing Egyptians. Israel saw in this event also the hand of God. This conviction is reinforced in the triumphal song of chapter 15.

Exodus 15

The knowledge that God sustained His people in the wilderness wanderings lies at the root of the 'Bread of Heaven' to which Jesus alludes in the New Testament.

Exodus.16.vv.1-15

Of enduring value in the Old and New Testaments is the giving of the Ten Commandments.

Exodus.20.vv.1-17

LEVITICUS

This is probably the book which finally deters those who set themselves the task of reading the unabridged Bible in its entirety.

Leviticus is an extension of the account of the Exodus events. The material it contains is for a modern Gentile reader often irrelevant. Accordingly, the rules concerning sacrifice and ritual purification are omitted and only a few passages are recommended for reading.

The most attractive teaching in this book is contained in the following passages.

Leviticus 19.vv.9-18, vv.33-35

Morality and concern for the poor and alien are here seen to arise out of the concept of a loving, caring Sovereign Lord.

Leviticus 23.vv.23-44

The festivals and Holy Days prescribed here and elsewhere in the Bible are of interest, especially the Day of Atonement (Yom Kippur) and the Feast of Booths (cf.*Neh.8.vv.13-18*) both of which are still honoured by modern Jews.

3

The laws regarding slavery are happily, and at long last, of little interest to modern readers.

NUMBERS

This book contains a mass of regulations which are not all relevant to a modern non-Jewish reader, but two brief passages commend themselves.

This brief but lovely passage known as the 'Priestly Benediction' is well loved by all Jews and Christians.

Numbers 6.vv.22-27

The commissioning of Joshua as the successor of Moses is of great interest, since it prefigures the practice of religious commissioning down through the history of Jews and Christians to the present day.

Numbers 27.vv.12-23

DEUTERONOMY

The book Deuteronomy which means 'Second Law (Giving)' describes the arrival of Israel on the borders of the 'Promised Land'. There Moses teaches them the statutes and ordinances of God and the book ends with the death of Moses after he has commissioned Joshua to succeed him.

The journey of 40 years is resumed under God's blessing.

Deut.1.vv.6-8 and 2.v.7

Moses foretells his death and urges his people to observe the Covenant God has made with His people.

Deut.4.vv.22-40

The Second Law Giving (see *Exodus.20.vv.1-17*) now follows.

Deut.5.vv.1, vv.6-21

A warning is given against faithlessness.

Deut.6.vv.4-13, and vv.20-25

God's love for His people is declared.

Deut.7.vv.7-13

God disciplines His people, and warnings are given against pride and lack of gratitude.

Deut.8.vv.5-20

What does God require? This is one of the loveliest Old Testament passages.

Deut.10.vv.12-15

'Do not forget these words of mind'. Aids to memory.

Deut.11.vv.18-21

The chapters that follow, concerned with pagan and ancient Jewish ritual, sabbatical years, punishments, penalties and rules of warfare are omitted, but a few of the laws concerning love for the poor and needy, and gratitude for God's gifts are retained.

Deut.23.vv.24-25, and 26.vv.1-11

The choice of life and death, blessings and curses form a fitting conclusion to Moses' warnings to his people.

Deut.30.vv.1-5, and vv.9-20

As Moses feels his life is drawing to a close, he appoints Joshua to succeed him as leader of the people.

Deut.31.v.23

An account of the death of Moses and a tribute to his role as Servant of God concludes the book of Deuteronomy.

Deut.34.vv.1-12

JOSHUA

The book Joshua describes the early stages of Israel's entry into the 'Promised Land'.

In a very fine passage we read of Israel's conviction that God had promised to grant them the Promised Land and that he would be an ever present help to their leader Joshua, provided that he remained loyal to God.

Joshua 1.vv.1-9

It is difficult, and probably impossible now, to verify the details of Joshua's campaigns, nor is it of great importance. One incident, however, is very interesting. However much the story may be exaggerated (the 'entire nation'), it is certain that the river Jordan was as liable to be dammed up as to flowing. Some such remarkable event appears to have happened as described in this passage and a memorial instituted to this saving event.

Joshua 4.vv.1-9

There follows an idealised account of the proportioning of the land among the tribes of Israel; but whereas we read here that the whole land of Canaan (Palestine) was conquered and settled, the book of 'Judges' makes it plain that the conquest was partial, piecemeal and of longer duration than Joshua's career.

Joshua's farewell speech, recapitulating God's saving acts, is a masterly summary of Israel's blessings and of warnings to them to heed their future conduct.

Joshua 21.vv.43-45, and 24.vv.14-18

JUDGES

As we have seen in the book of Joshua, there was in his days only a partial settlement of Canaan; for in this book we read of heroic exploits, frequent campaigns and miraculous deliverances in the troubled period following Joshua's death.

Many of the details of the story are manifestly legendary or historically improbable. For those reasons they are omitted, but religious insights of value are to be found, and these are included.

The 'Judges' were charismatic leaders who arose to deal with specific crises in this troubled period. There is a clearly perceived pattern running through the book, viz. Israel sins and is disloyal to God, - trouble befalls them in the form of invasion or oppression by their enemies round about them, - they call on God to deliver them, - God raises up from among them a 'Judge' (Deliverer) who rescues them, - a period of peace ensues (until the next cycle of misfortunes).

Judges 2.vv.11-19

After accounts of the colourful exploits by the Judges and of the near annihilation of the tribe of Benjamin, the book closes with the comment of *Judges 21.v.25* - "In those days there was no king in Israel; all the people did what was right in their own eyes" - a fitting introduction to the historical books of Samuel, Kings and Chronicles which continue the history of the loose confederation of tribes as they attempt to unite under kings who will act as a rallying point and lead them to victory over their foes.

Meanwhile, before Israel's story continues, we have the lovely story of Ruth with its setting in the Judges period (hence its position in the Old Testament canon).

RUTH

This lovely little book reflects some of the customs and way of life current in Israel in the Judges period, but it was probably written many years later as a gentle protest against the exclusive attitude towards non-Jewish people current in post exilic Judaism (cf. the book of Jonah).

In addition to giving a tender picture of love and concern for aliens, the poor and needy and for widows, the concept of racial purity is raised at the end of the book, where it is stated that even the greatly loved and revered King David inherited through Ruth the Moabitess his great grandmother Gentile blood! Had not God a purpose for Gentiles as well as for Israel?

I SAMUEL

We come now to the books of history - Samuel, Kings and Chronicles, which describe the emergence of the monarchy after the period of the Judges. All history is necessarily written from the standpoint of the writers, and in the case of Israel's history is written from a religious or theological viewpoint, i.e. God is in control of history : He is Sovereign Lord and King : weal and woe depend on the response of the nation to God. We see this "Deuteronomie" insight worked out in the narrative.

Samuel was the last and greatest of the Judges. His birth and dedication are described in a charming manner dear to Jew and Christian alike.

I Samuel 1.vv.1-28

The call of Samuel is another charming and popular account.

I Samuel 3.vv.1-21

During the period when Samuel 'judged' Israel, there was continual harassment from their Philistine neighbours; but in general they managed to hold them in check.

I Samuel 7.vv.11-17

It is perfectly understandable that a loose confederation of tribes relying on the rise of 'Judges' or champions in times of stress should foresee the need of a king to unite and lead them in their struggles with aggressive and marauding neighbours. Samuel, however, gave them a solemn warning in their demand for a king.

I Samuel 8.vv.1-22

Samuel agreed to the demand for a king and sought God's guidance in choosing and anointing Saul to be Israel's first king.

I Samuel 9.vv.1-21, and 10.v.1

The career of Saul as king began with great promise in successful campaigns against Israel's enemies round about; but the figure of Samuel continually haunted him for alleged acts of disobedience to the Lord. Finally Samuel is convinced that Saul is no longer fit to be king, and with God's guidance seeks out and anoints David, son of Jesse, in his place.

I Samuel 16.vv.1-13

The career of David abounds in colourful exploits, beginning with the account of the slaying of Goliath, a story which is very popular. One of David's followers Elhanan is reported in *2 Samuel 21.v.19* to have killed Goliath. Sometimes the deeds of his followers are ascribed to the king to enhance his reputation for gallantry; but despite that and the failings of David, he was, and still is, held in great honour as the 'Ideal King', faithful to his God.

David's popularity and his friendship with Jonathan, Saul's son, no doubt contributed to Saul's jealousy of David.

I Samuel 18.vv.12-16

Jonathan's friendship with, and loyalty to, David are proverbial, and illustrated in the account of Jonathan rescuing his friend from Saul's anger.

I Samuel 20.vv.30-42

David's respect for Saul as the 'Lord's Anointed' is illustrated in two stories:

I Samuel 24.vv.1-22 and 26.vv.1-25.

Throughout the troubled period of Saul's kingship, the Philistines remained a threat to Israel, and it was in battle against them that Saul and Jonathan his son died.

I Samuel 31.vv.1-3, and vv.7-13

II SAMUEL

This book continues the history of Israel under David as king. David lamented the deaths of Saul and Jonathan, but there was continual strife between the house of Saul and that of David until David's succession was consolidated.

Stories of intrigue, violence, treachery and bloodshed marred the reign of David. During his reign the ancient city of Jebus was taken and became, with varying fortunes, Jerusalem the capital city of Israel.

II Samuel 5.vv.1-10

Towards the end of his reign it appears that David wished to build a 'dwelling place' for God in Jerusalem, but through the prophet Nathan was dissuaded.

II Samuel 7.vv.1-29

The concluding years of David's reign were bitter for him. His own grievous sin in lusting after Uriah's wife, Bethsheba, and his treachery in encompassing Uriah's death caused him, at the rebuke of Nathan the prophet, to feel remorse for which he repented. Moreover the disorder in his own household, the rivalry of his sons, their indiscipline, scheming and immorality caused David great sorrow, which culminated in the death of Absalom, David's favourite son.

II Samuel 18.v.24 to 19.v.8

David's trust in God, shown in his 'Song of Thanksgiving' (Psalm 18) (whenever or by whomever written) is probably the basis for the ascription of the Psalter (the Psalms of David) to the great king.

II Samuel 22.vv.1-51

Knowing that his end was near, David spoke his 'Last Words', again showing his trust and confidence in God.

II Samuel 23.vv.1-5

A brief anecdote showing David in a very favourable light is given in this final chapter of the book.

II Samuel 23.vv.13-17

I KINGS

The book I Kings opens, as one might expect, with a succession struggle even before the death of King David. This was resolved in favour of Solomon, David's son by Bethsheba.

I Kings 2.vv.1-4, and vv.10-12

Solomon made a promising start to his reign, as his recorded dream shows.

I Kings 3.vv.3-29

Solomon gained a great reputation for wisdom among his own and neighbouring peoples, but his astuteness in judgement was offset by his tendency to adopt some of the idolatrous practices of neighbouring peoples and a luxurious life style - sins which the Chronicler of his own days and later generations accounted an offence to God and man. The greatest achievement of Solomon was the building of the Temple in Jerusalem.

I Kings 5.vv.1-18 and 6.v.1, vv.11-14

At the dedication of the Temple, Solomon is represented as offering up a prayer containing wonderful religious insights into God's nature and His ways with mankind.

I Kings 8.vv.27-34, and vv.41-61

The religious and secular offences of Solomon culminated in a division within the nation of Israel, with increasing animosity between 'Israel' in the north and 'Judah' (Jerusalem) in the south.

I Kings 11.vv.26-43, and 12.vv.1-20

At this point the detailed histories of 'Israel' and 'Judah' are omitted, because they are concerned mainly with power struggles, civil wars, antipathy between the north and south and religious offences such as can be found in any secular or religious history.

In chapter 17, however, we encounter a new dimension in Israel's religion, namely the rise of the great PROPHETS who in their relationship with God, with the royal household and with the common people wielded immense political and religious influence and are honoured as those who spoke out for God and the true faith of the Old and New Testaments.

I Kings 16.v.29 to 19.v.16

Elijah in his opposition to Ahab and Jezebel won a great victory for the true faith on Mount Carmel. In another confrontation with the royal house, he was destined to rebuke the king in God's name and to predict the death of Jezebel.

The book I Kings closes with the prophet established as a power to be reckoned with in the affairs of the nation, speaking out for God and rebuking without fear or favour all who transgressed God's will.

I Kings 21.vv.1-20

II KINGS

The book II Kings introduces us to the Prophet Elisha who in the 'still small voice' or 'sound of sheer silence' (*I Kings 19.v.12*), was designated Elijah's successor.

II Kings 2.vv.1-18

Many are the tales of Elisha's wonder working but included here are only several narratives which are of interest or religious value:

11

- Elisha at Shunem (*II Kings 4.vv.8-37*)
- Naaman the leper (*II Kings 5.vv.1-27*)
- The 'Heavenly Chariots' (*II Kings 6.vv.8-23*)

The book II Kings continues with a remarkable passage describing [A] the conquest of 'Israel' and their deportation by the Assyrians. The religious historian asserts that this was an act of judgement and entirely due to the nation forsaking the Lord their God. Only 'Judah' was left of the original tribes of Israel.

II Kings 17.vv.1-24

[B] Judah in the south, as we read in *II Kings 17.v19*, was similarly guilty, but spared for the time being. Later, however, in King Hezekiah's day Sennacherib, King of Assyria, captured all the cities of Judah, except Jerusalem which became a vassal of Assyria and paid tribute.

II Kings 18.vv.13-16

It was not long before Sennacherib again threatened Jerusalem; but King Hezekiah fortunately listened to the Prophet Isaiah, son of Amoz, who showed remarkable faith in God's power and will to defend the city.

II Kings 19.vv.15-34

The further history of Judah is taken up in the careers and teaching of the prophets. Before the book closes we have two important passages to consider; [A] The religious reforms of the young King Josiah, based upon the 'Book of the Law' (Deuteronomy? or part thereof?)

II Kings 22.v.1, and 23.v.25

[B] The danger from Assyria had passed; but Babylon had succeeded Assyria as the enemy from the north, and in the days of Jehoiakim, Judah was forced to pay tribute to King Nebuchadnezzar. His son Jehoiakin, however, decided to rebel against Babylon, but was forced into submission and the final catastrophe was yet to occur.

II Kings 24.v.10 and 25.v.12

'So Judah went into exile out of its land' (*II Kings 25.v.21b*). The further history of Israel is bound up in the books of the Old Testament Prophets and Writings.

I CHRONICLES

As its name suggests, this book abounds in lists and genealogies as it recapitulates the early history of Israel contained in the books of Samuel and Kings and, historically speaking, adds nothing of value to the former accounts.

When, however, we reach Chapter 16 we have, in addition to passages of praise, singing and dancing, a splendid introduction to the Book of Psalms. Here are to be found excerpts from Psalms 96, 105 and 106, praising God for all his wondrous gifts, his steadfast covenant with His people and His loving care.

I Chronicles 16.vv.8-36

The book closes with the end of David's reign, to whom is attributed a lovely passage of thanksgiving, blessing and dedication to God.

I Chronicles 29.vv.10-20

II CHRONICLES

As one might expect, the history of Israel continues in the second book of Chronicles. The magnificence and splendour of Solomon's court is emphasised, and much emphasis is laid upon the work of priests and Levites.

As in the book II Kings we read of the utter destruction of Jerusalem by the Babylonians; but an introduction is given to us of the 'glorious' event that ended the Exile of Israel in Babylon, namely the fall of the Babylonian Empire and the rise of the Persian king, Cyrus.

Whether the edict of Cyrus is historically and verbally accurate matters not; but it serves as a fit introduction to the post-exilic history of Israel contained in the later historical books Ezra, Nehemiah and the Prophets.

II Chronicles 36.vv.22-23

EZRA

This book takes up the history of Israel into the period we call 'Judaism'.

The dating of this book and its connection with that of Nehemiah that follows may be of concern to academics, but to the average Bible reader is of little consequence.

What really matters is that both books reflect a post-exilic period when, chastened by suffering, God's people, established once more in their own land, determine to be a people apart from the nations round about. An exclusive attitude characterises this period of the history and religion of Israel which we term 'Judaism'.

It is extremely doubtful whether King Cyrus made his edicts in the form given, but certainly permissions was granted for captive Jews to return and to restore the devastated city of Jerusalem.

Ezra 1.vv.1-7

The returning exiles determine to rebuild the 'House of God'.

Ezra 2.vv.68-69

Great emotion was experienced as the work of Temple rebuilding was begun.

Ezra 3.vv.1-13

Considerable opposition was experienced from Jerusalem's neighbours round about, as they contemplated a powerful city arising from the ashes of Jerusalem, but with God's help the returning exiles succeeded in completing the work of restoration and rebuilding.

Ezra rejoiced in the work accomplished, but was dismayed that the "Jews" (the returned exiles) had not kept themselves pure and separated from the peoples round about. No doubt he was haunted by the fear that they would be corrupted by contact with their neighbours. Here begins (or continues) that exclusive attitude that separates the Jew from the Gentile. Ezra prays and declares that foreign marriages must be dissolved. Although many hearts were no doubt made heavy, Ezra's decree resulted in the cleansing of Judah from foreign influences.

Ezra 9.v.1 to 10.v.5

14

NEHEMIAH

The book of Nehemiah supplements that of Ezra but also tells of the struggles of the returning exiles to rebuild and fortify the ruined city of Jerusalem, surrounded as they were by jealous and hostile neighbours.

Nehemiah 1.vv.1-11c to "Your name"

Despite plotting, treachery and threats, Nehemiah the Governor stirred up the people for the mammoth task of rebuilding, and with God's help the city's defences were rebuilt.

Nehemiah 6.vv.15-16

The rededication of the city, the public reading of the Law and thanksgiving to God for his mercies form a fitting climax to the work of Ezra and Nehemiah. The Feast of Booths was re-established, a memorial of the 'sojourn in the wilderness' (cf. *Leviticus 23.v.42*).

Nehemiah 8.vv.1-18

The book closes with long lists of Priests, Levites, Singers and ritual observances, followed by the enforcement of strict Sabbath observance and segregation of the 'Jews' (Israel's survivors) from Gentiles (non-Jewish peoples).

ESTHER

This book, popular among Jewish people, has as its background the period of the 'Medes and Persians' who succeeded Babylon as the next great power of the Middle East. No doubt there is a historical basis to the story of a Queen Esther who skilfully saved many of her Jewish compatriots from a massacre in 473 B.C. in the days of Xerxes I (King Ahasuerus in the text).

Suffice it to say that her success is commemorated in the Jewish Feast of 'Purim'.

JOB

The book Job is rightly regarded as one of the great masterpieces of the Old Testament. Many commentaries and scholarly treatises have been written upon it. Detailed interpretation of the book is beyond the scope of this guide to the Bible; but the book 'speaks for itself'.

It was written probably about 400 B.C. but the subject matter - that of innocent suffering and the right attitude of the creature to the Creator - is of perennial interest and importance.

Within the setting of a 'fairy tale' which is not exclusively Jewish (cf. Hariscandra of Egypt) we have some of the deepest theological probings of the Old Testament.

The book so nearly resembles a Drama that it may easily be read in this manner from the following Synopsis:-

1. Job is portrayed as an innocent God-fearing character, who suddenly suffers a series of terrible misfortunes, but yet retains his integrity and faith in God.

Job 1 and 2

2. Job gives vent to his sorrow.

Job 3

3. The first cycle of the speeches of Job's three friends and Job's impassioned reply.

Job 4 - 14

4. The second cycle of speeches and Job's reply.

Job 15 - 21

5. The third cycle of speeches from two of his friends and Job's reply.

Job 22 - 31

6. After Job's long speech (*Job 22-31*) there follows a speech from a certain "Elihu" regarded by some as an 'unnecessary interpolation', but in reality advancing the argument of the book greatly and contributing new and valuable insights into the mystery of God's ways with mankind.

Job 32 - 37

7. The climax of the book comes in chapter 38 when God Himself answers Job and overwhelms him.

Job 38 - 41

8. Job is overcome with shame and remorse and despises himself for his rashness in questioning the sovereignty and wisdom of God.

Job 42.vv.1-6

9. God now reproves the friends of Job, but commends Job himself. The 'fairy tale' beginning of the book is now rounded off in a 'happy ever after' manner.

PSALMS

Literally and figuratively at the very heart of the Bible we have the Psalter (the book of Psalms), a veritable storehouse of spiritual inspiration for Jew and Christian alike.

The Psalms have been so beloved by all the major Christian denominations that, with a few exceptions, we include them in this shortened Bible.

In some instances there are certain 'verses' in the Psalms that are omitted because they include thoughts of vengeance and cruelty, but we should not be surprised that the Jews sought vengeance upon their enemies, nor that they opened their hearts to God in prayers, telling Him not only what they desired but also telling Him what He should do!

Some Psalms (96, 105, 106) are omitted because they are included in the study of Deuteronomy.

There are may good commentaries and devotional books written on the Psalms, so that it is unnecessary to categorise them and to attempt to interpret them in this study. All who love the Psalms would agree that to a very large extent they speak for themselves.

Psalms

Book I Numbers 1 - 41

Book II Numbers 42, 43, 44, 46, 47, 48, 49, 50, 51, 57, 62, 63, 65, 67, 71

Book III Numbers 84 to 86

Book IV Numbers 90, 91, 92, 93, 95, 97, 98, 99, 100, 102, 103, 104

<u>Book V</u> 107, 111, 112, 113, 116, 117, 118, 121, 122, 123, 124, 125, 126, 128, 130, 131, 134, 137, 138, 139, 142, 143, 145, 146, 147, 148, 150

PROVERBS

As its title suggests, we have here a stock of wise, witty and often humorous sayings, which make up a collection of traditional folk-lore and religious teaching which ranges from pithy, sometimes cynical, often misogynous worldly wisdom to profound religious insights.

Not all of this material is native to Israel; for there are affinities with other Middle East 'Wisdom' literature. Several strands or sources may be detected by their style and subject matter. Here we have selected only a few representative passages.

The reputation Solomon gained for 'Wisdom' understandably accounts for the ascription of the book to him.

'Wisdom' is a popular concept in later Judaism sometimes so exalted in the writings of Israel as to become a prime attribute of the Almighty.

The passages selected emphasise that the 'fear of the Lord' is the beginning of 'Wisdom'.

Proverbs 1.vv.1-10, 2.vv.1-6, 3.vv.3-6, and vv.11-18

There follow now 28 chapters of sayings that contrast the characteristics and behaviour of the wise and foolish, the good and bad, the righteous and unrighteous; until the book ends with a passage well-beloved for its beauty and the honour it pays to womankind.

Proverbs 31.vv.10-31

ECCLESIASTES

The book Ecclesiastes with its keynote "Vanity, all is Vanity" is so imbued with the spirit of pessimism and gloomy determinism that we may wonder how it came to be included in Holy Scripture. Perhaps the concluding verse with its pious sentiment commended the book and gained its acceptance in the canon.

The worldly wisdom contained in this book does not usually attract those who, rejoicing in God's loving purposes for mankind, hold an optimistic world view.

There are, however, passages in this book which have a haunting beauty and contain genuine religious insights. We therefore cite the concluding verses of the book.

Ecclesiastes 12.vv.1-8

THE SONG OF SOLOMON

Unlike the sad book Ecclesiastes which precedes it, this book breathes an atmosphere of joy. The reason for this contrast is simply that the "Song" is a series of secular love songs associated with betrothal and marriage. Since it is included in Holy Scripture, some people have regarded it as a picture of the love of God for His people (the "bride" of God).

A popular and restrained example of the love song is occasionally found, but there are no explicit references to God or to religion.

Song of Solomon 2.vv.8-13

ISAIAH

We come now to books of prophecy, but it must be remembered that "prophecy" denotes not simply a foretelling of future events but also a declaration of God's ways with mankind and His purposes for them, read in the light of history past, present and future.

Many scholarly tomes have been written on the authorship, style and interpretation of the writings known as "Isaiah", but for our purposes it will suffice simply to distinguish between the prophet Isaiah of the earlier pre-Exilic period and the writing of Isaiah chapters 40 onwards, the prophet of the return from Exile and the subsequent period.

The book finds its unity in the concepts of Ethical Monotheism, of the creative majesty, dominion and inspired word of God, the God of all nations.

The prophet describes the sorry state of a rebellious nation and calls for repentance.

Isaiah 1.vv.1-31

In chapter 2 we read of God's sovereignty extending not only over Israel but also over Gentile (non-Jewish) people.

Isaiah 2.vv.1-22

In chapter 5 the prophet continues the theme of exile and destruction for a sinful nation.

Isaiah 5.vv.1-30

The call and willing acceptance of the prophet contrasts sharply with the reluctance so often shown by those whom God calls to His service.

Isaiah 6.vv.1-8

It has been customary for Christians to associate the "sign to Ahaz" with the birth of a Saviour "Immanuel" ("God with us").

Isaiah 7.vv.10-14

The "Christmas theme" recurs again in chapter 9.

Isaiah 9.v.2, vv.6-7

The prophet regards Assyria as a scourge in the hand of God to punish His rebellious people.

Isaiah 10.vv.1-16

The prophet foresees destruction coming upon his people, but he also introduces the theme of hope - the idea of a "saved remnant" of his people in whom the future of the nation is bound up.

Isaiah 10.vv.20-25

Chapter 11 begins with another passage in which Christians see prefigured the Christ who saves His people, one who brings universal peace and restores the exiles.

Isaiah 11.vv.1-11

This section of Isaiah ends appropriately with a joyful song of praise to God for His goodness.

20

Isaiah 12.vv.1-6

We now have oracles (not always in chronological order) describing the fate of Israel's neighbours and enemies at God's hands, culminating in a harrowing picture of the "Day of the Lord" when He brings wholesale destruction upon the earth. The final judgement is declared.

Isaiah 24.vv.1-11, and vv.21-23

After the "Day of Judgement" God is represented as reigning over the world from Jerusalem. For this the prophet raises a joyful song of praise and thanksgiving, extolling the might and majesty of God and exulting in the favours bestowed upon the remnant of His people.

Isaiah 25.vv.1-10

Scarcely, however, have the shouts of joy at Israel's deliverance died away, when we find the prophet foretelling another visitation in wrath - the siege of Jerusalem (Ariel) the city of a rebellious people.

Isaiah 29.vv.1-4, and vv.13-14

Disaster will surely come; yet, says the prophet, the Lord is a God of mercy and forgiveness if you turn to Him.

Isaiah 30.vv.8-26

After the impending horrors of the siege of the city, says the prophet, a new age will dawn. In beautiful and memorable language the prophet describes this bliss.

Isaiah 35.vv.1-10

There follows a detailed and interesting account of the taking of the cities of Judah and of threats to Jerusalem from the Assyrian King Sennacherib. Isaiah advises King Hezekiah of Jerusalem to stand firm, for God would save His own city.

Isaiah 36.vv.1-10, vv.13-21 and 37.vv.1-7, vv.15-35

The city was saved at least for a while but eventually it was besieged by the Babylonians who succeeded the Assyrians as the dominant power in the

Middle East. Great was the fall of the city, and the inhabitants were taken into exile.

At chapter 40 in this "Isaianic collection" of writings we have a sudden change of mood. Some of the finest writing in the Old Testament is contained in this and the following chapters.

The exile in Babylon, which was not of long duration, is drawing to a close, and the Jews are about to return to rebuild Jerusalem and to resume their life in Judah - and great is their joy.

The prophet sees the hand of the Almighty in the events of the day. God is Sovereign Lord, the Holy One, Creator, Redeemer, Tender Shepherd.

Isaiah 40.vv.1-31

The prophet ascribes to God's action the fall of Babylon and the rise of Cyrus the Persian who is to permit the return from exile. He is God's "agent".

Isaiah 41.vv.1-4, vv.8-20

We come now to a series of "Servant Songs", lovely passages about which many commentators have written. Some regret that they cannot with certainty identify the "Suffering Servant", but this should not cause undue concern, since Christian piety has ascribed many of the facets of these complex figures to Jesus Christ, whose role and characteristics defy neat categorisation.

Isaiah 42.vv.1-25

The theme of joy at God's deliverance and His ever-watchful care of His people is continued. Nature itself shares in Israel's blessings and God's forgiveness.

Isaiah 43.vv.1-25

In chapter 44 the "Servant Song" theme is again taken up with a call to confidence in the Lord the Redeemer.

Isaiah 44.vv.1-6, vv.21-28

In a very fine passage God's sovereignty is set forth and Cyrus is described as the "Anointed" (Messiah, Christ) who unwittingly fulfils God's redemptive purpose for His people.

Isaiah 45.vv.1-25 and 48.vv.17-20

God's Servant has suffered, says the prophet, but now he has a mission not only to Israel but also to the ends of the earth.

Isaiah 49.vv.1-13, and 51

The prophet describes the coming of the messenger with good news.

Isaiah 52.vv.7-10

One of the greatest "suffering servant" passages has also been seen by Christian piety as prefiguring the redemptive suffering of Jesus Christ.

Isaiah 53.vv.1-12

This section of the immediate post-Exilic prophecies ends with a lovely invitation to all mankind to share in the joy of Zion and the gift of life abundant.

Isaiah 55.vv.1-13

It is difficult to believe that the chapters which follow come from the pen of the prophet responsible for chapters 40 - 55. Again we have a change of emphasis and subject matter in the Isaianic prophecies. Instead of the paeans of praise, we have a legalistic strain, a concern for Sabbath keeping and ritual. It is difficult to date these prophecies accurately, but probably they come from a period when religious practices are being re-established (and also corrupted). The writer looks beyond the narrow confines of Judaism (the post-Exilic religion).

Isaiah 56.vv.6-8

The denunciations of disobedience and licentiousness contained in these chapters would suggest that either the material is pre-Exilic or that there has been a rapid deterioration in the religious life of the newly established Judaism.

Isaiah 58.vv.1-14 and 59.vv.1-21

Again we have a change of mood. A happier and more optimistic note is sounded. Israel is to be the source of light to the world because she is God's own people, the "beloved bride" of God. Zion is to be truly blessed.

Isaiah 60.vv.1-22, 61.vv.1-11, 62.vv.1-12 and 63.vv.7-9

JEREMIAH

In the troubled period leading up to the Exile in Babylon, the prophet Jeremiah pronounced his oracles. His name is often associated with pessimism; but it would probably be truer to say that he was a realist, as well as a man of deep spiritual insight.

Jeremiah's Call and Commission show him to be one who did not readily respond (as did Isaiah of Jerusalem) to God's call. A deeply sensitive man, he shrank from the prospect of confrontation with his people, who would not agree with his conviction that Jerusalem's calamities were an inevitable and just retribution for the nation's sins. Nevertheless he found God's call overwhelming.

Jeremiah 1.vv.1-19, 2.vv.1-13, and v.19

Yet, says the prophet, God desires to show mercy if only His people will repent; otherwise calamity will overwhelm the land.

Jeremiah 3.vv.12-22, and 4.vv.15-29

The prophet despairs of finding even one just person in Jerusalem. Rich and poor alike have forsaken the Lord. Yet, says the Lord, there will be mercy shown to a remnant of the people.

Jeremiah 5.vv.1-5, vv.18-31

The religious practices of the Temple are no talisman against evil. The prophet grieves over the sin and sufferings of his compatriots.

Jeremiah 7.vv.1-11, 8.vv.18-21 and 9.v.1

Jeremiah represents his people as acknowledging their sin, and pleads their cause but is bidden to forbear. False prophets are deceiving the people with predictions of peace and priests are abetting them.

Jeremiah 14.vv.7-21

The prophet plumbs the depths of despair in his unpopularity but is assured of God's protection and His love for all who love and serve Him.

Jeremiah 15.v10, and 17.vv.7-16

In a well known parable or similitude we learn that as a potter shapes and reshapes his vessels, so can the Lord deal with His people.

Jeremiah 18.vv.1-17

The unpopularity of Jeremiah continues and increases, despite his pleas on his people's behalf. The enmity of the priesthood is incurred and violent hands are laid upon him; but he stoutly repeats his message of impending doom.

Jeremiah 18.vv.18-20, and 20.vv.1-6

In his grief the prophet complains to God about the unpopularity and suffering that his oracles have brought upon him in his obedience to the Lord.

Jeremiah 20.v7-18

Having denounced false prophets and a corrupt priesthood, Jeremiah now inveighs against the royal house, which should have been a shepherd to God's people.

Jeremiah 23.vv.1-6

The culmination of Jeremiah's prophecy was a sentence of death passed upon him on the grounds of treason, but common sense and Ahikam's help saved him for the time being.

Jeremiah 26.vv.1-19, v.24

Despite his personal danger, Jeremiah continues to counsel submission to Babylon before disaster should strike the land, warning his people that failure to submit was contrary to God's will.

Jeremiah 27.vv.8-15

One of the most optimistic oracles of Jeremiah was the letter he sent from Jerusalem to those who in an earlier deportation had become exiles in Babylon.

Jeremiah 29.vv.1-14

This is followed by an even more joyful oracle - the promised restoration of all who have been taken into exile.

Jeremiah 30.vv.1-22, and 31.vv.1-17

With the restored community God will make a new Covenant based upon individual responsibility.

Jeremiah 31.vv.27-34

Jeremiah was so confident that God would permit the exiles to return from exile that he bought some land outside Jerusalem where a besieging army of the Babylonians was encamped.

Jeremiah 32.vv.1-15, vv.36-41 and 33.vv.7-8, vv.10-11

There follows an interesting account of how Jeremiah's scroll was destroyed, but through his pertinacity and the good offices of his Scribe Baruch his oracles were preserved for posterity.

Jeremiah 36.vv.1-32

Not only was Jeremiah's scroll nearly destroyed, but he himself was beaten, imprisoned and consigned to a muddy pit, from which he was rescued by a servant of the king with the latter's connivance. Meanwhile the city continued in a state of siege.

Jeremiah 37.vv.1-21 and 38.vv.1-28

Jeremiah's predictions of impending doom were justified. The city of Jerusalem fell to the Babylonians. Jeremiah's life was spared and he was allowed to remain with the poorest people of the land in the ruins of Jerusalem under Gedaliah who was appointed by the Babylonians as Governor over them.

Jeremiah 39.vv.1-14 and 40.v.6

Some time after these events Gedaliah was murdered by a certain Ishmael. Fearful of the consequences of this deed, many of the leading Jews fled to Egypt, taking with them the reluctant Jeremiah, who continued in Egypt to pronounce oracles of wrath and destruction upon the fugitives who, he declared, had again disobeyed the Lord and incurred His wrath. So ends the

"Word of the Lord" from the voice of Jeremiah and the pen of his faithful Scribe Baruch.

Jeremiah 44.vv.1-25

Of the death of Jeremiah nothing is known for certain. The book ends, as we might expect, with oracles concerning neighbouring peoples and with a prediction that Babylon will fall and Jerusalem rise again.

Jeremiah 50.vv.1-10 and vv.17-20

LAMENTATIONS

The book Lamentations has been ascribed to Jeremiah. Whether the ascription is correct it matters not, for the theme - the desolation of Jerusalem - is consonant with Jeremiah's oracles and his grief over the stricken city.

Lamentations 1.vv.1-5

The bitter lament over Zion continues, but eventually a note of faith, hope and love is sounded.

1 How lonely sits the city that once was full of people! How like a widow she has become, she that was great among the nations! She that was a princess among the provinces has become a vassal.

2 She weeps bitterly in the night, with tears on her cheeks; among all her lovers she has no one to comfort her; all her friends have dealt treacherously with her, they have become her enemies.

3 Judah has gone into exile with suffering and hard servitude; she lives now among the nations, and finds no resting place; her pursuers have all overtaken her in the midst of her distress.

4 The roads to Zion mourn, for no one comes to the festivals; all her gates are desolate, her priests groan; her young girls grieve, and her lot is bitter.

5 Her foes have become the masters, her enemies prosper, because the Lord has made her suffer for the multitude of her transgressions; her children have gone away, captives before the foe.

EZEKIEL

Ezekiel who prophesied to the Exiles in Babylon was a mystic visionary whose spiritual experiences are not easy to understand; but he had a valuable contribution to make to Israel's faith.

We read first a passage in which we encounter the figures that the Christian Church has adopted as symbols of the New Testament Gospel writers (a human being, a lion, an ox and an eagle) and the glory of the Almighty upon His throne. The word 'mortal' (man) in this version is a way of rendering Ben Adam (Son of Man) in earlier versions of the Bible.

Ezekiel 11.vv.14-20

In an inspired insight the prophet declares that the age-old conviction of Israel that God deliberately "visits the sins of the fathers upon the children" is to be replaced by a sense of <u>personal</u> responsibility.

Ezekiel 36.vv.22-36

One of the most powerful images the prophet gives us is that of the "Valley of Dry Bones" with its spiritual awakening. Whether we use the interchangeable words "wind", "breath" or "spirit", (ruach) the meaning of this passage is crystal clear.

Ezekiel 37.v1-14, v24-28

The book closes with detailed instructions for the rebuilding of the Temple in Jerusalem and the ordinances and ritual to be observed in its worship.

DANIEL

The book Daniel purports to describe events which took place in Babylon after the fall of Jerusalem. The stories it contains have all one purpose - to show that God cares for and protects those who are faithful and put their trust in him in times of difficulty and danger.

Although the history of religions amply prove that those who are persecuted for their beliefs are <u>spiritually</u> protected and "saved" by their constancy and faith, yet it is also clear that God does not always bring their <u>physical</u> sufferings to a happy issue.

Most scholars believe that this book is a kind of "tract for hard times", i.e. a treatise produced at a time of religious persecution to encourage and strengthen those who are (figuratively) cast into a "burning, fiery furnace" or being "cast among lions". The stories have captured the imagination of many artists, readers and writers down through the ages and such stories as "Belshazzar's Feast" and the "Writing on the Wall" are very popular.

The chronology of the book is obscure, but towards the end we come across a passage which links the book closely with the other prophecies of the Exile period.

Daniel 9.vv.4-19

The purpose of the book, however, is clearly to nerve and strengthen those who (probably at the time of the tyrant Antiochus Epiphanes, the Greek) were facing persecution for the faith; and the (deliberate) obscurities for the uninitiated were intended to safeguard those who produced or read this "underground newspaper".

HOSEA

The prophet Hosea likens the relationship between Israel and her God to that of a wife to her husband. The prophet declares that although Israel has proved faithless, yet God in His tender love and faithfulness cannot and will not cast her off, but having disciplined her will restore her to His favour.

Hosea 2.vv.19-20

A grim picture is painted of Israel's sins, but the prophet urges repentance in a lovely passage which speaks of God's pardon and loving kindness.

Hosea 4.vv.1-3, and 6.vv.1-6

having further elaborated his account of Israel's (Ephraim's) sins the prophet in a tender passage represents God as filled with compassion for His erring people, longing to forgive and restore them.

Hosea 11.vv.1-4, and vv.8-11

The prophet ends this short book with a further plea to Israel to return to the Lord, assuring them that He is a God of forgiveness and loving kindness.

Hosea 14.vv.1-7

JOEL

The little book of Joel, so seldom read, contains some very interesting insights and some fine racy writing. The assertion that God uses Israel's foes to execute judgement upon His erring, faithless people runs through this, as well as the other, prophetic books.

What is probably the unique message of this book is first the idea of the wholesale destruction and disaster that overwhelms not only the people, but also the natural environment; secondly the theme of judgement the "Day of the Lord" so vividly foretold; thirdly the pouring out of God's Spirit upon those who repent and are redeemed - a theme taken up in the New Testament (*Acts 2.vv.17-21*).

Joel 1.v.1 to 2.v.29

AMOS

The prophet Amos tells us much about himself and about the shortcomings of Israel the northern kingdom, which he, a man of Judah in the south, was called by God to denounce. His message is one of uncompromising judgement upon a people who lack a sense of social justice, religious purity and compassion. The "Day of the Lord" will overwhelm them.

Amos 1.vv.1-2, and 3.vv.1-2

The prophet is so concerned with the Day of Wrath that he says little about God's forgiveness; though he does hint at it in chapter 5.1v14-15.

Amos 5.vv.1-2, and vv.6-24

The theme of "uprightness" is taken up in a vision of Amos in which the "upright" Lord declares His judgement upon Israel. The oracles of Amos, however, so vexed the religious authorities of the north that they sought to banish the troublesome prophet through the priest Amaziah, who was himself greeted by rebuke and condemnation from Amos.

Amos 7.vv.7-17

Amos predicts not only a famine affecting the land and the people but also speaks of a "famine" of the word or guidance of God.

Amos 8.vv.1-12

There is no firm evidence that the book originally ended at chapter 9 verse 11, but the gracious ending of the book hardly accords with the stern warnings and predictions of the dark "Day of the Lord". Perhaps it is an addition designed to mitigate the gloomy predictions, but its (undoubtedly genuine) note of hope is in keeping with the many predictions found elsewhere in the prophetic writings of pardon and restoration for God's people.

Amos 9.vv.11-15

OBADIAH

The word "Obadiah" means "Servant of the Lord". Who he was we cannot tell.

This little book takes us back to the quarrel of Jacob and Esau in the Patriarchal Period. The sustained hostility of the descendants of these two brothers is here elaborated into a solemn warning to the Edomites (Esau) not to gloat over Israel (Jacob) in their day of calamity, for the "Day of the Lord" comes upon all the nations and Zion will be saved.

Obadiah 1.vv.11-17

JONAH

As we discovered in a study of Ruth, Nehemiah and Ezra, the returning exiles were urged to keep themselves pure and free from Gentile contacts. This was considered necessary in order to preserve the purity of Judaism, but among those of a more liberal viewpoint there was probably a recognition that non-Jewish people too had a part to play in God's purposes for mankind.

It may well be that this little book is a gentle protest, for in it God is represented as rebuking "Jonah" (= "Dove", another name for Israel) for his lack of concern and compassion for the Gentile city of Nineveh.

Jonah 1.v.1 to 4.v.11

MICAH

The contribution which Micah makes to the prophetic insights of the Old Testament consists largely in his wider vision of God's purposes for mankind.

After inveighing against Israel's sins, the prophet foresees a bright future.

Micah 1.v.1 and 4.vv.1-5

Christian piety has always seen the birth of Christ prefigured in the oracle (quoted in *Matthew 2.v.6*) of Chapter 5.vv.2-5.

Micah 5.vv.2-5

One of the first oracles of Micah is his description of true religion and what God requires of the worshipper.

Micah 6.vv.6-8

Despite his optimism, Micah was overcome with grief at the current state of affairs in Israel; but the complaint gives way to the vision of a bright future in which the surrounding nations come to worship Israel's God, the God of compassion and steadfast love.

Micah 7.vv.1-20

NAHUM

The style of this little book is racy. One can hear even in translation the clamour of war, the rush of horses and warriors as the prophet describes the ruin of Nineveh the city so hated by those enslaved by Assyria. Knowing how ruthless a foe Assyria was to her neighbours, one can understand the prophet's excitement and joy at the prospect of that city's downfall. This, says the prophet, is God's judgement upon a cruel foe and His promised salvation for His people.

Nahum 1.vv.1-15, and 2.vv.1-13

HABAKKUK

Like the book of Nahum, this book is also concerned with the ruthless Assyrian foe, but it also has fresh insights to contribute. It begins with a complaint about God's seeming indifference to the plight of His people.

Habakkuk 1.vv.1-13

The prophet is reassured by God's answer that salvation will surely come.

Habakkuk 2.vv.1-4

The book ends on a joyful note of trust in God's goodness.

Habakkuk 3.vv.17-19

ZEPHANIAH

Whereas the majority of the Minor Prophets concentrate upon Israel or Judah, this prophet appears to enlarge the scene and envisages a cosmic judgement, the "Day of the Lord". The book opens with overtones of the Noah story; but soon concentrates on Israel's sin and judgement. Nevertheless the thought of a universal "Day of Wrath" is still envisaged.

Zephaniah 1.vv.1-16, v.18 and 2.vv.1-3

The concept of a disciplining of the nations is taken up again in Chapter 3 but Jerusalem is still to be paramount among them all.

Zephaniah 3.vv.8-20

HAGGAI

After the return from exile in Babylon, despite the initial excitement and anticipation, and perhaps because of the enormity of the task of rebuilding the Temple, some of the enthusiasm appears to have evaporated and to have been followed by a period of inaction, disillusionment and spiritual torpor.

Haggai the prophet forcibly reminds his people of their priorities, that the worship of God comes first and stirs them up to the task of rebuilding the ruined Temple in Jerusalem. Only so, says he, can they hope to prosper.

Haggai 1.v.1 to 2.v.9

ZECHARIAH

The prophet Zechariah, like the prophet Ezekiel, was a mystic visionary, whose oracles are not easily understood. The first vision of the watchers' horses bears a message of grace and comfort for the returning exiles; the earth is at peace, God is returning to His people. Zion will again prosper.

Zechariah 1.vv.7-17

The prosperity of Zion is emphasised again in the vision of the man with the measuring line. there is no need to build walls around the city, for God Himself will be its shield and defence. The prophet also predicts that other nations will join with Israel in the worship of her God. God is the God who acts!

Zechariah 2.vv.1-13

Several of the visions of Zechariah, though colourful and interesting, are omitted because they add little to the spiritual content of the book, but we return to a lovely passage which again speaks of God's abiding presence in Zion and of peoples of other nations coming to worship Israel's God. The highlight of Zechariah's prophecy is the concept of the universal appeal of Israel's God!

Zechariah 8.vv.3-13

The book of Zechariah ends with oracles some of which the Christian Church has applied directly to the coming of Jesus Christ in His role as the humble "Prince of Peace" (*Matthew 21.v.5*) on Palm Sunday .

Zechariah 9.vv.9-10

MALACHI

The name Malachi means "My Messenger". Whoever the prophet may have been, his little book, ending the Old Testament in traditional Bibles, makes a fitting transition to the New Testament.

Several of the oracles of Malachi point forward to the New Testament both in Christian piety and also in the thoughts and words of Jesus Christ, His contemporaries and the Gospel Writers (*Mark 1.v.2*).

The first of these predictions is the coming of "My Messenger" to "prepare the way of the Lord".

Malachi 3.vv.1-7

After many admonitions to preserve the statutes and ordinances of the Lord, the prophet declares that Elijah will appear before the "Day of the Lord" arrives. Jesus himself (in *Matthew 11.v24*) appears to equate Elijah with John the Baptist and the Christian Church sees in the latter not a "reincarnation", but one who comes in the spirit and power of the great prophet.

Malachi 4.vv.1-5

The most significant link, however, contained in this book which so aptly links the Old and the New Testament is paradoxically the last word "CURSE". For Christian people God's "curse" is not simply averted, but transcended by the blessings of the Gospel the "Good News" of the New Testament.

INDEX TO CONTENTS OF THE NEW TESTAMENT

New Testament Passages

THE FOUR GOSPELS

We include the Four Gospels exactly as they stand.

There are innumerable books and commentaries on the Four Gospels, and although we wish the Gospels to "speak for themselves", as the Word of God has always done, we have included from passages from the Gospels with a brief commentary on the theme of each passage, 52 general commentaries for the 52 weeks of the year (A passages) and 20 on Feast and Fast Days (B passages). These are in the second part of this work, "We Preach Christ".

Matthew chapters 1 - 28

Mark chapters 1 - 16

Luke chapters 1 - 24

John chapters 1 - 21

ACTS

The book of the Acts of the Apostles relates how the early Christian church began to spread from Jerusalem after the giving of the Holy Spirit - the "Whitsun" or "Pentecost" experience.

The outline of the history is retained in the portions selected from this book; certain passages, however, are omitted and only the more interesting and essential highlights of this remarkable story are included.

The book begins with the account of Jesus' Ascension into heaven.

Acts 1.vv.1-14

Since Judas Iscariot had in remorse taken his own life, it was decided that another should be appointed to complete the number of the Twelve

Apostles. Peter quite naturally became spokesman and leader of the Apostles.

Acts 1.vv.21-26

The amazing event of Pentecost is described in full.

Acts 2.vv.1-8, vv.12-24, vv.32-33, vv.36-47

The power of the Holy Spirit is seen at work in the healing of a lame man by Peter and John.

Acts 3.vv.1-21

The healing miracle resulted in the imprisonment of the two Apostles, but after making a spirited defence of their action they were released.

Acts 4.vv.1-31

Peter becomes pre-eminent in the Apostolic band and many converts are made, so that the religious authorities again take action against Peter and John; but they were released on the advice of the wise Gamaliel.

Acts 5.vv.12-42

As the influence of the Early Church began to increase, it was found necessary to appoint helpers. This was done by laying on of hands with prayer. Among these was Stephen, a most able and God-fearing man, who in his zeal and condemnation of the religious authorities brought down upon himself wrath and eventually martyrdom.

Acts 6.vv.1-15, and 7.vv.54-60

Present at the scene of Stephen's martyrdom was a certain Saul who led a campaign of persecution against the infant Christian community, but later became "St. Paul", one of the foremost champions of the Church.

Acts 8.vv.1-3

Nothing daunted by the persecution, Philip, the companion of Stephen, went to the city of Samaria where his message and healing powers met with great success.

Acts 8.vv.4-13

The success of Philip in Samaria was so great that the Apostles Peter and John were sent into Samaria to build upon his work. Meanwhile Philip was divinely guided to travel south towards Gaza where he met with and baptised an Ethiopian official of the royal house.

Acts 8.vv.26-40

The well-known and well-attested story of Saul's conversion to "the Way" (of Christ) is now recorded, and peace now descends on the infant Church.

Acts 9.vv.1-31

Again we return to accounts of Peter's travels and his healing miracles.

Acts 9.vv.32-43

An event of great significance now takes place. Whereas up to this time the Good News had been imparted solely or mainly to Jews and "God-fearers" (Gentiles attracted to Israel's God), Peter now learns that there is a place for Gentiles in God's purposes.

Acts 10.vv.1-48

Not without setbacks, but slowly and surely, the Church accepted Gentiles into their Christian community and Barnabas enlisted the aid of Saul in this work of conversion.

Acts 11.vv.19-26

Again the interest centres upon Peter who, arrested by King Herod, had a second miraculous escape from prison.

Acts 12.vv.1-19, vv.24-25

Barnabas had enlisted the help of Saul in evangelising the Gentile world and he and Saul (now <u>Paul</u>) visited Cyprus. Among the Gentiles they had considerable success, but met with opposition from the Jewish community. Paul, who was chief spokesman, so angered the Jews of Iconium that he was stoned and left for dead but survived the ordeal and returned to Antioch where he and Barnabas had been commissioned.

Acts 14.vv.19-28

A controversy over whether Gentile converts to Christianity should be required to accept and observe all the ritual laws of Judaism vexed the Early Church, but was resolved in favour of the Gentiles and a letter sent to Antioch to confirm the decision reached.

Acts 15.vv.22-35

While Paul (with Timothy and Silas as his companions) was spreading the 'Good News' in Asia Minor, he received a vision in which he was urged to cross from Asia Minor to Macedonia to bring the Gospel to Europe. At this point in the narrative the writer (St. Luke?) apparently joined in the mission.

Acts 16.vv.6-15

There follows now the account of an incident which brought Paul and Silas into great danger from the Gentiles.

Acts 16.vv.16-40

After his escape from the hostility of the Gentiles, Paul faces hostility from the Jews of Thessalonika, but, leaving Silas and Timothy, Paul was despatched by his friends to Athens.

Acts 17.vv.1-15

In Athens Paul addressed the Assembly with a defence of what he believed and won some support.

Acts 17.vv.16-34

Leaving Athens, Paul visited Corinth where Silas and Timothy rejoined him. Here he had a mixed reception and encountered opposition from some Jews but by God's grace escaped the danger and returned via Jerusalem to Antioch, his starting point.

Acts 18.vv.1-22

Nothing daunted by the trials and tribulations of his second expedition, Paul set off again to revisit the infant Churches of Asia Minor. His work in Greece (Achaia) was consolidated by a certain Apollos.

Acts 18.vv.23 to 19.v.8

After his prolonged stay in Asia Minor, Paul resolved to revisit Greece and Jerusalem and to visit Rome. A serious disturbance in Ephesus very nearly thwarted all Paul's plans. but having been rescued from this new danger, Paul left for Macedonia.

Acts 19.v.23 to 20.v.1

After a three month stay in Greece strengthening the young Churches, the news of a plot against him caused Paul to decide to return to Jerusalem. His farewell speech to the Elders of Phesus on his journey homeward is a very moving passage.

Acts 20.vv.17-38

Despite warnings and pleas from his friends, Paul persisted in his determination to visit Jerusalem, where he was warmly welcomed; but within a week he was seized and nearly lynched by a crowd stirred up by some Jews from Asia on the charge that he was subverting the Jewish faith. Rescued from this peril by the Roman tribune, and guarded from his Jewish adversaries by Roman soldiers, Paul made a spirited defence of his beliefs and teaching. As soon, however, as he mentioned his conversion and commission to the Gentiles, rioting broke out again.

Acts 22.vv.17-22

The tribune, learning that Paul was a Roman citizen and therefore liable to bring trouble upon those who had unjustifiably arrested him, released Paul and arranged for him to make a further defence of his conduct before a Council of the Jews.

Acts 22.vv.23-30

With great skill, Paul turned to his advantage a reference to the "resurrection of the dead" in his sermon for his defence. In the violent disturbance that followed between the Pharisees and Sadducees, the tribune managed to save Paul from the clutches of the Jews and protect him in the barracks.

Acts 23.vv.6-11

Learning that some of Paul's enemies had sworn to hill him, the tribune in his perplexity sent Paul under armed escort to Felix the Governor in Caesarea.

Acts 23.vv.12-15

Within a week the High Priest and several of his party arrived from Jerusalem in Caesarea and before Felix laid serious charges against Paul. In a masterly speech in his defence, Paul rebutted the charges, declared his innocence and was for two more years granted a limited degree of freedom, chiefly because of the perplexity of Felix.

Acts 24.vv.1-26

Felix was succeeded as Governor by a certain Festus who became responsible for the fate of Paul, whose enemies hoped to have him ambushed and killed on his way to Jerusalem. Festus asked Paul whether he wished to be tried in Jerusalem, but Paul made the momentous decision "I appeal to the Emperor". This was the privilege and right of those who were full Roman citizens and sealed his fate for better or worse. Henceforward it was incumbent upon the authorities to ensure that decision about Paul's future would be made in Rome.

Acts 24.v.27 and 25.vv.1-12

While Paul remained in Caesarea, Festus received a visit from King Agrippa who said that he would gladly hear what the prisoner Paul had to say in his defence of his belief and conduct. Arrangements were made accordingly.

Acts 25.vv.13-27

The defence of Paul before Agrippa is a wonderfully succinct summary of Paul's career as a Christian and made a profound impression on King Agrippa - but the die had been cast. Paul was destined to go to Rome.

Act .26.vv.1-32

The journey to Rome, fraught with dangers and near disaster, is a very exciting and moving story and since it illustrates so well the faith of Paul we include it in its entirety.

Acts 27.v.1 to 28.v.16

Paul's reception in Malta, in Italy, and in Rome was cordial but when he delivered his message in Rome there was, as might be expected, scepticism shown by some of the orthodox Jews. Nevertheless, he was able to spend there at least two years preaching the Good News of Jesus Christ.

Acts 28.vv.17-31

ROMANS

This important letter of St. Paul sets forth his teaching on "Justification by Faith", that is, by <u>faith</u>, and not by works of the Law, we receive the Grace of God and are made acceptable to Him. The arguments the Apostle uses are at times abstruse and difficult to follow outside the context of Jewish thought. There are, however, many helpful and inspired passages in this letter and these are included for study.

After a rather lengthy and involved greeting and explanation of his reasons for writing, St Paul (quoting from the Old Testament book of Habakkuk.2.v2) announces the theme which he then elaborates, "It is by faith that we gain (Eternal) Life".

Romans 1.vv.1-21

The Apostle now declares that all mankind, whether Jews or Gentiles, stand before God guilty of sin, but through faith in Jesus Christ are "justified" ("acquitted" or "made acceptable" to God).

Romans 3.vv.10-26 and 4.vv.7-8

St Paul describes the blessings which stem from the sacrificial death of Christ.

Romans 5.vv.1-11

St. Paul sets forth the theme of spiritual life and death and the power of the indwelling Spirit. He concludes with a wonderful affirmation of faith - a passage well known and well beloved.

Romans 6.vv.1-11, 8.vv.26-27, vv.31-39

Life in the Spirit has its practical consequences for all who embrace it and its gifts are to be used to God's glory.

Romans 12.vv.1-21

Jesus' summary of the Law of Love is reproduced by the Apostle coupled with an urgent summons to be active and alert for "whether we live or die we are the Lord's".

Romans 13.vv.8-14, 14.vv.7-9

The letter ends with greetings to friends in Rome and an ascription of honour and glory to God.

Romans 16.vv.25-27

I CORINTHIANS

This letter of St. Paul was sent to the Church that he founded in Corinth. Sadly divisions have arisen in the Christian congregation, and the Apostle is anxious that there shall be no rifts among them. As their

"Founding Father", St. Paul lays down strict codes of behaviour for this Church, dealing in detail with matters such as sexual immorality, lawsuits, marriage bonds, slavery, food laws, the worship of idols and the subordination of woman to man. Most of this ethical teaching is omitted here, but there are some wonderfully deep religious insights contained in this letter.

The letter begins with an expression of faith in his converts and an appeal not to be disunited. The Apostle declares that the message he delivered is one of simplicity, yet of spiritual power.

I Corinthians 1.vv.1-17, and 2.vv.1-13

St. Paul returns to the theme of disunity and quarrelling and emphasises that those who founded the Church are but servants of God, building upon Christ as the foundation.

I Corinthians 3.vv.5-11, vv.16-23

After giving detailed instructions about the conduct of Christians as in the introduction to this letter, St. Paul ends with an important passage referring to the institution of "Holy Communion".

I Corinthians 11.vv.23-26

The Apostle now gives details of spiritual gifts and their use in building up the "Body of Christ" - His Church.

I Corinthians 12.vv.1-31

One of the best known and best loved passages of this letter is St. Paul's "Hymn to Love".

I Corinthians 13.vv.1-13

The Apostle now deals with the phenomena of prophecy and "speaking in tongues".

I Corinthians 14.vv.1-5

The important Chapter 15 contains a summary of the gospel message which St. Paul delivered to the Corinthian Church, and his teaching about the Resurrection of the Dead.

I Corinthians 15.vv.1-28

The letter ends with the Apostle's final injunction and greetings.

I Corinthians 16.vv.13-14, vv.20-21, v.24

II CORINTHIANS

St. Paul's second letter to Corinth contains some valuable autobiographical details and religious insights.

After greeting his friends in the Church, the Apostle tells of his and his companions' suffering for the sake of the gospel and his consolation in Christ.

II Corinthians 1.vv.1-11

Despite the hardship and heartache, St. Paul declares his unswerving devotion to the ministry and the proclamation of the gospel.

II Corinthians 4.vv.1-12

The Apostle now describes the new life in Christ and the Christian role in reconciliation.

II Corinthians 5.vv.17-21, and 6.vv.1-10

St. Paul encourages the Church in charitable giving, citing for example the generosity of God and His Son Jesus Christ.

II Corinthians 8.vv.1-9, and 9.vv.6-15

The Apostle enumerates the hardships he has endured for the sake of the gospel and his anxiety for the young churches.

II Corinthians 11.vv.24-28

St. Paul concludes his letter with a final appeal and the "Trinitarian Grace" which has become so much a part of Christian worship.

II Corinthians 13.vv.11-13

GALATIANS

Some commentators regard this letter as an abbreviated form of the "Gospel" (Good News) that St. Paul delivered in his letter to the Romans. There is some truth in this; but it does contain some valuable additions. Probably it was the original short form of the Epistle to the Romans.

After his introductory greeting, the Apostle deals directly with a serious problem vexing the churches of Galatia. There were some in the Galatian church who sought to undermine and mislead the converts who accepted the "pure" gospel revealed directly to the Apostle by Jesus Christ.

Galatians 1.vv.1-12

The problem centred around the question that still vexed some sections of the church - whether Gentiles should be required to accept the whole Law of the Jews before being accepted as Christians. St. Paul repeats the teaching he gave in the letter to Rome of "Justification by Faith".

Galatians 2.vv.15-21, and 4.vv.4-7

St. Paul, making a sharp distinction between the good principle of "Spirit" and the evil principle "Flesh" (unregenerate), describes the difference that living by the Spirit makes in the lives of true believers.

Galatians 5.vv.19-25, and 6.vv.1-2, v.7-10, v.18

EPHESIANS

The authorship of this letter is a matter of dispute. Beginnings and endings of letters may easily mislead, since letters were so rare and valuable, and probably often adapted to suit particular times and places. The authorship is a matter of slight importance; the important thing is that the letter has been preserved and bears the authority of St. Paul, and some very valuable teaching.

The introduction to this letter is very impressive as it sets forth God's eternal and redemptive purposes for His people.

Ephesians 1.vv.1-23, and 2.vv.1-10

The writer elaborates the theme that Jew and Gentile, once separated, are now one in Christ.

Ephesians 2.vv.13-22, and 3.vv.14-20

This new found unity in Christ lays upon all the duty of living lives worthy of one's calling and the exercise of one's spiritual gifts.

Ephesians 4.vv.1-32, and 5.vv.1-20

The writer deals with some of the moral problems of his day, but ends the letter with a well known and stirring challenge couched in terms of spiritual warfare.

Ephesians 6.v.5, vv.10-23

PHILIPPIANS

The tone and contents of this letter amply attest the confidence that inspired St. Paul in his imprisonment for the gospel.

Philippians 1.vv.1-30

The Apostle enjoins humility upon the community of believers after the example of Christ, who laid aside his heavenly attributes to become man.

Philippians 2.vv.1-11

Despite his sufferings and the uncertainty of his earthly prospects, St. Paul not only bids his fellow Christians to have peace and joy, but knows and experiences them himself. He commends the generosity shown by the Church on his and others' behalf.

Philippians 4.v.1, vv.4-9, vv.15-23

COLOSSIANS

St. Paul writes tenderly to the Christians in Colossae with whom he is well pleased because of their steadfast faith and love.

Colossians 1.vv.1-23

The Apostle refers to the church as the "Body of Christ" and declares his devotion to the upbuilding of it and the imparting of the "mystery" of the gospel.

Colossians 1.vv.25 - 2.v.7

St. Paul tells his readers of the kind of life that is in conformity with the acceptance of life in Christ.

Colossians 3.vv.1-17, and 4.vv.2-6, and 8-11

I THESSALONIANS

St. Paul in the introduction to this letter commends very warmly the faith of the Thessalonian converts; here we have a tender picture of the Apostle gently nurturing them in the faith.

I Thess.1.vv.1-10, 2.vv.1-17, and 3.vv.6-13

Having praised the converts for their faith and conduct, the Apostle urges them to even greater efforts in holy living.

I Thess.4.vv.1-12

There was apparently doubt in the minds of some in the church about what would happen to the souls of those who died before the coming of

49

the "Day of the Lord". St. Paul attempts to reassure them with a verbal picture of the Day of the Lord. Although to many these thought forms may seem naive and improbable, no doubt they were comforting to those vexed by the problem.

I Thess.4.v.13 - 5.v.11

The letter ends with an appeal to the church to hold fast the faith in purity of life in love, joy and peace; a very lovely benediction concludes the letter.

I Thess.5.vv.12-28

II THESSALONIANS

Whereas the second letter to the Thessalonian church begins (as the former) with commendation, it soon becomes apparent from the fiery language that the church is suffering persecution and hardship. St. Paul reminds his readers that, as he explained in IThessalonians, the "Day of the Lord" is coming with vengeance.

This letter was intended as a word of encouragement and consolation to those who were suffering and looking forward to their vindication.

Having unburdened himself of the predictions of imminent destruction of the powers of darkness and violence, the Apostle renews his praise and encouragement of the church.

II Thess.2.vv.13-17

The Apostle closes with a plea to the church to be steadfast in the faith and to live blameless lives.

II Thess.3.vv.1-5, v.13, vv.16-17

I TIMOTHY

St. Paul writes a letter of encouragement to his helper whom he describes as his "child in the faith".

50

In the letter the Apostle gives detailed instructions on matters of church order and discipline, some of which do not apply today in the Christian church and are therefore omitted, but the most valuable material is his personal advice to Timothy himself.

I Timothy 1.vv.1-7, vv.12-17 and 2.vv.1-7

Timothy is exhorted to make good use of his gifts in teaching and leading a blameless life as an example to the Church, observing the duties that fall to his lot as a "man of God" and warning against the danger of a love of money.

I Timothy 4.vv.1-16, and 6.vv.6-26

II TIMOTHY

In his second letter to his "beloved child" St. Paul commends the faith of Timothy and encourages him to rekindle the gift of ministry which he received, reminding him of his responsibilities and privileges as a teacher of God's people.

II Timothy 1.vv.1-14, and 2.vv.1-3, vv.22-26

The Apostle refers to the persecutions that are the inevitable lot of those who follow Christ, but exhorts Timothy to shun evil and to remain firm in the faith and to treasure the scriptures that are the word of God.

II Timothy 3.vv.12-17, and 4.vv.1-5

TITUS

St. Paul appears to have given his assistant Titus a formidable task to perform in Crete to judge from his opinion of the Cretans expressed at the beginning of his letter!

The Apostle enumerates the failings of the Cretans and urges Titus to discipline them with severity, but he is, as always, careful to stress that personal example in godly living is of paramount importance in those who teach and instruct.

Titus 1.v.4, and 2.vv.7-8, vv.10-15

The tone of the letter becomes more pacific and conciliatory in tone as it proceeds, and allowances are made for the Cretans, as the Apostle recalls that he and his companions were not always in the past God-fearing and blameless in their behaviour before receiving the gift of the Holy Spirit.

Titus 3.vv.1-7, v.15

PHILEMON

This charming little letter of St. Paul forms a fitting conclusion to his "personal correspondence".

The details of Onesimus ("Useful" v.11) absconding from his master are neither known nor of importance, but the Apostle's advocacy of him is a very lovely trait in St. Paul's character.

Philemon vv.1-25

HEBREWS

The authorship of Hebrews is a matter of conjecture. There are plenty of commentaries dealing with this and the other difficult problems raised by the letter; but only those passages intelligible and relevant to the modern Christian are included in this study.

Christian religious doctrines and insights are in this letter contrasted and compared with Old Testament faith and substantiated by a skilful use of Old Testament "proof texts" but the most valuable passages for Christian study are those that can stand in their own right apart from Old Testament background.

The writer begins his letter with a very fine description of Jesus as God's "First and Last Word" to His world.

Hebrews 1.vv.1-3, and 4.vv.12-16

A considerable portion of this letter is devoted to teaching about faith. The writer argues very persuasively for the importance of faith in the religious life. There is an interesting parallel in this letter with St. Paul's reference to *Habakkuk 2.v.2*, which the Apostle uses to such effect in Romans, and this writer uses as a starting point for his treatise on faith.

Hebrews 10.vv.32-38, and 11.vv.1-3

There now follows an impressive list of God's servants in Old Testament times who served Him in faith.

Hebrews 11.v.32 to 12.v.2

The letter ends with a blessing often associated in the church with the season of Easter.

Hebrews 13.vv.20-21

JAMES

This letter addressed to Jewish Christians dispersed in the Mediterranean area has been subjected over the years to considerable adverse criticism, but we select the gems embedded in it and let them speak for themselves.

As Jesus taught, prayer to be effective should be offered with faith and conviction.

James 1.vv.5-8

God is the source of all giving and generosity.

James 1.v.17

James defines pure religion in a pragmatic manner as did the Old Testament prophets.

James 1.vv.19-27

A false and unhelpful distinction is often made between "faith" and "works" but in the context of James's words, one may perceive that the distinction is more apparent than real!

James 2.vv.14-18, v 26

James warns against the unbridled tongue with its attendant dangers.

James 3.vv.9-12

The writer commends the wisdom that comes from above.

James 3.vv.13-18

James ends his letter with practical advice for godly living and the treatment of those who are suffering, emphasising the power of prayer.

James 5.vv.13-16

I PETER

This letter of St. Peter, abounding in passages of great beauty and spirituality, is reproduced in full with the exception of a brief passage.

The church he is addressing is one which has already suffered persecution and is even then suffering. He seeks to bring encouragement and consolation to his readers by assuring them that Christ who suffered is with them in their sufferings.

I Peter 1.v.1 to 2.v.25, 3.vv.8-17, 4.vv.1-19 and 5.vv.1-14

II PETER

In his second letter St. Peter shows that he has come to terms with his impending death and wishes to exhort and encourage his readers before his departure.

The Apostle warns his readers against those who subvert the truth and deny their Master Christ.

II Peter 1.vv.1-21, and 2.vv.1-3

St. Peter reminds his readers that they must pay attention to the sacred words of the Prophets and Apostles.

The "Day of the Lord" may be delayed, but it will surely come in God's good time. The Apostle uses the imagery current in his day for the terrible "Day of the Lord", and the new order that is to succeed it.

II Peter 3.vv.1-4, vv.8-13

I JOHN

The first letter of John with its overtones of the Fourth Gospel needs no commendation or explanation, for it speaks for itself as the "Word of Life", even as the Gospels do.

1John 1-5

II JOHN

The second letter of John does not have such close affinity with the Fourth Gospel as the former letter does. It is difficult to ascertain who the "Elder" John may be. Commentators may propound theories about him and the "Elect Lady" (a Church?) but such considerations are of little importance. The message is plain "Beware of false prophets, deceivers and Antichrists!".

II John vv.1-13

III JOHN

The third letter of John is a personal letter addressed to an individual Gaius who was probably a disciple and fellow worker of the Elder (as Timothy was of St. Paul, and described as "his child").

Although the details and circumstances of this letter are scanty, the picture they give us of the early Church is very much what we would expect.

III John vv.1-15

JUDE

The little letter of Jude casts a dark cloud upon the picture of the early Church with its description of the forces arrayed against the Church; but it ends with an air of confidence and hope, and an ascription of blessing to God.

Jude vv.1-4, 12-13, 17-21, 24-25

REVELATION

The book Revelation describes mystic visions of a prophet or "seer" who claims to have foreseen the events which would take place in the coming of the "Day of the Lord" - judgement of all mankind in the "Last Day".

The language of the book is in places colourful (to say the least) and many of the thoughts expressed are repugnant to modern readers, especially the condemnation of the "Scarlet Lady" (Rome). These passages and the more lurid descriptions are therefore omitted but the sequence of events is retained in the text.

The book opens with a paean of praise and messages to the seven churches of Asia Minor.

Revelation 1.vv.1-11

The messages to the Churches are in the form of a "visitation" in which they are severally commended for their fortitude, patience, steadfast faith, repudiation of heresy and lover - or condemned for their lukewarm attitude, failure to repent, toleration of heresy, and warned of impending persecution and judgement.

This section ends with a lovely invitations to open the door to the Christ who stands and knocks.

Revelation 3.vv.19-22

There follows a series of visions which have close affinities with those of Ezekiel and other mystic visionaries. The first is of God in glory and majesty.

Revelation 4.vv.1-8

The next vision is of Jesus Christ, the only one worthy to open the judgement scroll of God.

Revelation 5.vv.1-14

A vision follows of the redeemed in heaven.

Revelation 7.vv.9-17

The hatred of Rome (for which was substituted the name "Babylon") suggests that following the persecution of Nero's day, relations with that city were at a low ebb for the early Christian church; and the jubilant prediction of the fall of that city is portrayed by language reminiscent of Isaiah and Jeremiah and all who rejoiced over Babylon's downfall.

After the pouring out of the "bowls of the wrath of God" on the earth and its inhabitants, the seer foresees a new heaven and earth and a new Temple in the new Jerusalem.

Revelation 21.vv.1-7, vv.22-26

In conclusion the writer gives a happier picture describing the water and the tree of life which God provides. He ends with a plea to Jesus Christ to hasten the day of His "Second Coming".

Revelation 22.v.19, v.21

We Preach Christ

Reflections on some Gospel passages - General themes

A1 GOOD NEWS

St. Luke 7.vv.18-23

~The disciples of John reported all these things to him. So John summoned two of his disciples and sent them to the Lord to ask, "Are you the one who is to come, or are we to wait for another?" When the men had come to him, they said, "John the Baptist has sent us to you to ask, "Are you the one who is to come, or are we to wait for another?"". Jesus had just then cured many who were blind. And he answered them, "Go and tell John what you have seen and heard: The blind receive their sight, the lame walk, the lepers are cleansed, the deaf hear, the dead are raised, the poor have good news brought to them. And blessed is anyone who takes no offence at me.~

The word translated "preach" in many versions of the Bible is better rendered as "Bring Good News", for that is what the original Greek word means. It is the word from which we derive "Evangel" and "Evangelism" and is the same word that St. Mark uses in the opening words of his Gospel, "The beginning of the good news of Jesus Christ, the Son of God".

It is the duty and high privilege of all Christian people to declare and share the good news - but how do we accomplish this? Consider the following account from the life of St. Francis:

It is recorded of St. Francis that he once promised to take a young Novice of the Order on a preaching tour in the neighbourhood. After visiting, helping and praying for several people who were in distress, they returned homeward; whereupon the young man, greatly perplexed, enquired of him, "When are we going to start the preaching?". "My brother", said the Saint, "we have been preaching all the time".

There are some who think that preaching means ordination and a pulpit to proclaim the word of God, not realising that all Christians are the "priesthood of all believers", and that the way in which we live, think and speak is, by the power of the Holy Spirit, a witness to the love of God and the salvation wrought by Christ.

All Christian people are called to witness in the world. It is for Christians an inescapable duty and a high privilege to witness; indeed we should feel like Jeremiah *(Jer.20.v9)* "a burning fire shut up in our bones" if we do not so witness; for as St. Paul said,

"Woe is me, if I preach not the Good News" *(ICor.9.v16)*

I like this little story immensely because, as I look back over my life, I am reminded of so many "unspoken sermons" - acts of love towards me, prayers offered for me, compassion shown to me which have spoken more eloquently than words could ever have done. I treasure the memories of so many loving souls who can never have known how, by their deeds as well as words, they have "preached" to me and drawn me into the love of Christ.

A2 ASKING

St. Luke 11.vv.1-13

~Jesus was praying in a certain place, and after he had finished, one of his disciples said to him, "Lord, teach us to pray, as John taught his disciples". He said to them, "When you pray say: Father, hallowed be your name. Your kingdom come. Give us each day our daily bread. And forgive us our sins, for we ourselves forgive every one indebted to us. And do not bring us to the time of trial".

And he said to them, "Suppose one of you has a friend, and you go to him at midnight and say to him, "Friend, lend me three loaves of bread; for a friend of mine has arrived, and I have nothing to set before him". And he answers from within, "Do not bother me; the door has already been locked, and my children are with me in bed; I cannot get up and give you anything". I tell you, even though he will not get up and give him anything because he is his friend, at least because of his persistence he will get up and give him whatever he needs.

So I say to you, Ask, and it will be given you; search, and you will find; knock, and the door will be opened for you. For everyone who asks receives, and everyone who searches finds, and for everyone who knocks, the door will be opened. Is there anyone among you who, if your child asks for a fish, will give a snake instead of a fish? Or if the child asks for an egg, will give a scorpion? If you then, who are evil, know how to give good gifts to your children, how much more will the heavenly Father give the Holy Spirit to those who ask him!".~

"Ask, and you will receive".

"Is this so?", we say. Does God always answer prayer? "Yes", says the true believer. All prayer is answered. But in what way is it answered?

There is often heartbreak in asking for those things you deem good and in accordance with God's will and finding prayer "not answered".

Only by knowing how Jesus himself prayed can we resolve the problems of prayer life.

Jesus prayed for hours in solitude. Prayer for him was being especially aware of the presence of God, being still before him, making his requests known to God, but all in the context of "Thy will (not mine) be done" for he trusted (as he assures us) that God hears and cares and answers.

The answer God gives may be "Yes", because it is not only his will but for the good of those who pray - and who knows better than God?

The answer may not be what we like, as in Gethsemane, but God's "No" is accepted by Jesus in the context of "Thy will be done". If God in his infinite love, compassion and wisdom says "No", it will still be hard to accept; but we know that God knows better than we do what is ultimately our highest good.

The answer may be "Wait". This "wait" may be for a day or two, a year or two - perhaps a lifetime? Sometimes we can look back over the years and by hindsight realise that God's "Wait" was for our good.

In His wisdom and love God says "Yes", "No" or "Wait", but as Jesus taught us we must persevere in prayer, not to "wear God down" by our importunity, but to assure him and ourselves that we truly desire his loving kindness and his purpose and direction in our lives.

Jesus gives us the pattern prayer.

1. The Our Father

We pray first for the things God wants.

Our Father. We acknowledge that all are his children. Perhaps one of the reasons why so much prayer seems unanswered is that we are selfish?

Hallowed. We need to recover (if we have lost it) reverence for God, for nature and for mankind made in the image of God.

Kingdom. Do we and does the world acknowledge the sovereignty of God in our lives?

2. Material Needs

We pray for our daily bread, but why do we need to ask if he gives it anyhow? We ask because we are totally dependent on his generosity and love.

We pray not for _my_ but _our_ daily bread and we remind ourselves that it will not be bread for all his children if we refuse or forget to give and share with others.

3. Spiritual Gifts

We ask for forgiveness for we all stand in need of reconciliation, pardon and peace.

We ask that our temptations may not be too severe for we know our frailty.

"Deliver us from evil" is a heartfelt plea, for there is so much evil around us and within.

Ask, and you will receive.

A3 CENTURION

St. Luke 7.vv.1-10

~ *After Jesus had finished all his sayings in the hearing of all the people, he entered Capernaum. A centurion there had a slave whom he valued highly, and who was ill and close to death. When he heard about Jesus, he sent some Jewish elders to him, asking him to come and heal his slave. When they came to Jesus, they appealed to him earnestly, saying, "He is worthy of having you do this for him, for he loves our people, and it is he who built our synagogue for us". And Jesus went with them, but when he was not far from the house, the centurion sent friends to say to him, "Lord, do not trouble yourself, for I am not worthy to have you come under my roof; therefore I did not presume to come to you. But only speak the word, and let my servant be healed. For I also am a man set under authority, with soldiers under me; and I say to one, "Go", and he goes, and to another, "Come", and he comes, and to my slave, "Do this", and the slave does it." When Jesus heard this he was amazed at him, and turning to the crowd that followed him, he said, "I tell you, not even in Israel have I found such faith". When those who had been sent returned to the house, they found the slave in good health.~*

Christians, agnostics and atheists all live by faith - faith in the ordered processes of nature, the "natural laws" that govern the universe, belief in things we can't prove, e.g. laws of gravity and the observed effects of things on people, but for religious people faith means trust, not in propositions and theories or things, but faith in a Person.

I read recently of a blazing house into which all who tried to enter were driven back. On a window sill high above the ground stood a little petrified girl who had escaped through the window. A crowd of distressed neighbours outside the house urged the little one to jump, but she refused until her father pushing to the front, opened his arms and called her name and shouted "jump!". She did and was saved, for she knew he was one to be relied on.

In *Jeremiah 32.vv.6-15*, we read of Jeremiah buying a field on which the besieging enemy was encamped, in the faith that God would in the future liberate the land.

In *Galatians 3.vv.6-9*, we have a reference to Abraham, the "Father of Faith", taking God at His word.

In *Luke 7.vv.1-10*, what a wonderful commendation the Centurion received from Jesus, "I have not found so great faith, no not in Israel" (where presumably he had grounds for expecting it).

What sort of man was this Centurion?

First he was a Roman, a Gentile not a Jew. His rank was roughly equivalent to that of Regimental Sergeant Major in the British Army probably a tough and hardened campaigner but he desired healing for his slave.

The Roman attitude to slaves was shown in the advice of Cato and Varro to farmers - "In the Spring look over your tools and slaves and discard any useless or badly worn" (slaves too!).

The Centurion was presumably a "God-fearer" with Jewish friends and attracted to Israel's God. He shows a humble respect for Jesus.

His faith was amazing, for he did not ask Jesus to come to his home but believed in Jesus' power and authority embodied in his "WORD".

The power of the divine "word" is described by Isaiah, "So shall my word be that goeth forth from my mouth ... It shall not return to me empty but shall accomplish that which I purpose and prosper in the thing for which I sent it"

(Isaiah 55). St. John says, "The Word became flesh and dwelt among us" *(John 1.v.14)*.

The Centurion knew that distance was no object. The universe is vast, yet God cares for all individuals.

Despite the incredible vastness of time and space Christians know that Christ is nearer than thinking or breathing. They know too that "all things are possible to those who have faith".

We put our faith in a person as did the Centurion. That person is none other than Jesus who is one with the Father who gives to His people, healing, pardon and peace.

A4 THANK YOU

St. Luke 17.vv.11-19

~ *On the way to Jerusalem Jesus was going through the region between Samaria and Galilee. As he entered a village, ten lepers approached him. Keeping their distance, they called out, saying, "Jesus, Master, have mercy on us!". When he saw them, he said to them, "Go and show yourselves to the priests". And as they went, they were made clean. Then one of them, when he saw that he was healed, turned back, praising God with a loud voice. He prostrated himself at Jesus' feet and thanked him. And he was a Samaritan. Then Jesus asked , "Were not ten made clean? But the other nine, where are they? Was none of them found to return and give praise to God except this foreigner?". Then he said to him, "Get up and go on your way, your faith has made you well". ~*

Shakespeare: *"Blow, blow thou winter wind/Thou art not so unkind/As man's ingratitude/Thy tooth is not so keen/Because thou art not seen/Although thy breath be rude/"*.

We all know the piercing cold of winter wind and we all loathe ingratitude, for it bites like a cold wind and fills us with dismay.

How often we hear the reaction. "Well! after all I've done ... I'll never ... That's the last time ..."

In *St. Luke 17.vv.11-19* we hear of Jesus healing ten lepers of whom only one (and he a Samaritan, an outsider politically and religiously) returned to give thanks for his healing.

We feel shocked and scandalised by this inability or unwillingness to say "thank you".

The nine demonstrated how easy it is to gain what we want and to give no further thought to the Giver (for all healing comes from the Father). Perhaps they had not realised it was God's gift? Perhaps they were too excited or too shy? We don't know, but we know Jesus was concerned about their ingratitude.

The one who returned to give thanks demonstrated a loving and grateful heart.

And what of us? Do we always take the trouble to say thank you? When we go abroad do we ensure that if we have no other word in our vocabulary we at least know "thank you" in our hosts' tongues? Do we remember God when ill and forget Him when we are made whole? All too often are we not unthinking unthankful people who take for granted God's gifts?

Or do we thank God daily for our food in grace before meat? and Harvest time? Do we thank God for the ability to walk, for our eyes to see the beauty of the created world, for our ears to hear music and conversations, our tongues to speak, the sense of smell?

Do we thank God for families and friends? for his providence and never failing presence in our lives - in sorrow and in joy?

Someone, a confirmed atheist, once said, "What a lovely day this is - if only there were a God to whom I could say "Thank you" for it!"

A short while ago I had occasion to wait for someone at a local hospital. As I often do on such occasions, I went into the Chapel to sit at the table, to read the Chapel literature, to pray and meditate. As I sat there a young man came into the Chapel. When he saw me, he slowed down perceptibly, as if not sure whether he should be there. Knowing that people use the Chapel to pray for themselves and others, I did not look towards him respecting his privacy. After a few minutes he prepared to go and passed quite close to me. Simply to be friendly I asked him, "All well?". He beamed all over his face and said, "Yes, thank you. I came in to say thank you, I've just come from the Maternity Ward where my wife has given birth to our first baby - a little girl". "All has gone well?" I asked. "Yes", he replied. "It's a lovely thing", I said, "to come and say thank you for this gift. I happen to be a Priest (for I wore no clerical collar) I would like to say "thank you" with you and for your wife and child". "I'm afraid", said he, "that I probably shouldn't be here because I don't attend Church, though I believe in Jesus Christ". "Where better", I said, "than here in

Chapel, thanking God for the gift?" We spoke for a little while longer to our mutual joy and parted with happy memories of a joyful encounter.

When we come to Church as Christian people we meet together to say thank you for the greatest gift of all - the gift of God's only Son. The Greek word for thanksgiving is "Eucharistia". We come to Eucharist or Holy Communion to say thank you to God for all his love and blessings bestowed upon us.

A5 MOURNING

St. John 14.vv.1-6

~ *"Do not let your hearts be troubled. Believe in God, believe also in me. In my Father's house there are many dwelling places. If it were not so, would I have told you that I go to prepare a place for you? And if I go and prepare a place for you, I will come again and will take you to myself, so that where I am there you may be also. And you know the way to the place where I am going". Thomas said to him, "Lord, we do not know where you are going. How can we know the way?". Jesus said to him, "I am the way, and the truth and the life. No one comes to the Father except through me".* ~

Blessed are those who mourn ~ really?!

What on earth (literally) did Jesus mean?

The word "mourn" is almost exclusively used of sorrow caused by the death of one we love. Moreover the word "blessed" in some inept translations is given as "happy" making confusion worse confounded. How can you understand this? So far from being "blessed", many mourners may become bitter about life, angry at God or with others, never able to overcome self-pity, overwhelmed by mourning and tears.

How often I have read these words in a funeral service and wondered how they sound when addressed to those who are beside themselves with grief, remembering the mutilated body of a dear one suddenly killed by a drunken driver, the wasted body of one who died a painful death, the little cot-death, the child cut short in her prime with leukaemia. The "natural" concomitant to mourning and tears is often bitterness, self-pity, self-hate, depression, keeping a stiff upper lip but inwardly being filled with more rage and depression than we can possibly handle; repressing feelings which may perhaps years later come to the surface and cause a pathological state of neuroses and black depression.

On the other hand, to mourn, that is, to give vent to our sorrow, may indeed be "blessed" because it allows for the grace of tears to begin the process of grieving and the long painful process of healing the deep wound caused by our loss.

The verse ends "for they shall find comfort". Humanly speaking, in a truly Christian setting who ever has lacked a shoulder to cry on, an arm around the shoulders? God gives us one another to be a comfort to us.

On the spiritual level, Psalms, Scripture and Christian experience testify to the presence of God in our affliction. The Christ who wept at the grave of Lazarus knows our sorrows, is with us in our pain, will never leave us or forsake us.

Mourning, however, is not simply what we do at the death of others for we mourn when we see the cruelty and stupidity of people in their behaviour towards one another, and we mourn for our own folly and wickedness when we consider the appalling mess we make of our lives, the mess our children possibly make of theirs, the mess that society in general certainly makes of its life, the world's sin and error, the piling of arms, the injustice, the lack of compassion around us.

Jesus lamented over Jerusalem and there is much for us to lament, but if we truly mourn, that is take to heart, view with compassion the sorrows of the world and our own, we do indeed by the grace of God receive comfort and know that we are ever in the love of God.

A6 PRODIGAL FATHER

St. Luke 15.vv.11-32

~ Jesus said, "There was a man who had two sons. The younger of them said to his father, "Father, give me the share of the property that will belong to me". So he divided his property between them. A few days later the younger son gathered all he had and travelled to a distant country, and there he squandered his property in dissolute living. When he had spent everything, a severe famine took place throughout the land, and he began to be in need. So he went and hired himself out to one of the citizens of that country, who sent him to his fields to feed the pigs. He would gladly have filled himself with the pods that the pigs were eating; and no one gave him anything. But when he came to himself he said, "How many of my father's hired hands have bread enough and to spare, but here I am dying of hunger! I will get up and go to my father, and I will say to him, "Father, I have sinned against heaven and before you; I am no longer worthy to be called your son; treat me like one of your hired hands". So he set off and went to his father. But while he was still

far off, his father saw him and was filled with compassion; he ran and put his arms around him and kissed him. Then the son said to him, "Father, I have sinned against heaven and before you; I am no longer worthy to be called your son". But the father said to his slaves, "Quickly, bring out a robe - the best one - and put it on him; put a ring on his finger and sandals on his feet. And get the fatted calf and kill it, and let us eat and celebrate; for this son of mine was dead and is alive again, he was lost and is found!". And they began to celebrate.

Now his elder son was in the field; and when he came and approached the house he heard music and dancing. He called one of the slaves and asked what was going on. He replied, "Your brother has come, and your father has killed the fatted calf because he has got him back safe and sound". Then he became angry and refused to go in. His father came out and began to plead with him. But he answered his father, "Listen! For all these years I have been working like a slave for you, and I have never disobeyed your command; yet you have never given me even a young goat so that I might celebrate with my friends. But when this son of yours came back, who has devoured your property with prostitutes, you killed the fatted calf for him!". Then the father said to him, "Son, you are always with me, and all that is mine is yours. But we had to rejoice, because this brother of yours was dead and has come to life; he was lost and has been found". ~

One of the characteristic traits of Christian people is their habit of telling one another stories, sometimes over and over again. This is something that they derive from their Founder, the greatest storyteller of all time. One of the greatest and most popular of Jesus' parables is the "Prodigal Son".

There are many ways in which story telling enriches the lives of Christian people, apart from the obvious entertainment value. Possibly the most important and valuable is self-identification with the characters of the story. The story we are considering is a splendid example of this.

The so-called Prodigal Son of the parable, who becomes a wastrel as the story progresses, began by seeking what many high-spirited youths desire - a break from home, travel and independence. Having received a share of his father's wealth, he led a life of luxury and debauchery until all his resources were exhausted. Having experienced want, misery and a guilty conscience about his way of life, he determines to return home and show heartfelt repentance, trusting that he may obtain at least mercy. His reception by his father who "killed the fatted calf" in his joy at receiving his son safely home exceeded all his hopes and expectations.

Truly the boy had been prodigal and wasteful with his riches, but the one who was truly prodigal in the sense of "lavish" and "bountiful" is the father who lovingly forgives and welcomes back his son. Christian people readily identify with the son because they know they stand in the need of forgiveness and love but none can identify with God the Father in his "prodigality", indeed many might more readily kill the son than the "fatted calf"!

The elder brother who bitterly resented the father's reception of the younger son is one with whom it is easy to identify. "It's not fair!" we hear him say, and he has at least some of our sympathy, until perhaps we remind ourselves that he had remained secure in his home. His service may have been joyless and he may well have been envious of his brother's seeming good fortune when he made the break with home and enjoyed the freedom of the world, but he needed the father to remind him that compassion, love and forgiveness transcend worldly pain and pleasure.

A7   PERSECUTION

St. John 16.vv.1-11

~ *Jesus declared, "I have said these things to you to keep you from stumbling. They will put you out of the synagogues. Indeed, an hour is coming when those who kill you will think that by doing so they are offering worship to God. And they will do this because they have not known the Father or me. But I have told you these things so that when their hour comes you may remember that I told you about them. I did not say these things to you from the beginning, because I was with you. But now I am going to him who sent me; yet none of you asks me, "Where are you going?". But because I have said these things to you, sorrow has filled your hearts. Nevertheless I tell you the truth; it is to your advantage that I go away, for if I do not go away, the Advocate will not come to you; but if I go, I will send him to you. And when he comes, he will prove the world wrong about sin and righteousness and judgement: about sin, because they do not believe in me; about righteousness, because I am going to the Father and you will see me no longer; about judgement, because the ruler of this world has been condemned." ~*

As St. Polycarp (mid second century AD) was on his way to martyrdom, he was urged by his enemies to recant, to deny Christ and thereby save his life. His reply was, "Eighty and six years I have served Him and He has done me no harm, how then can I deny my King who has saved me?". In this same spirit died many of the Christian martyrs.

We are bidden to pray for courage, strength and steadfastness in the face of persecution and suffering for the Gospels' sake. Since, however, few of us

Christians in the Western World have suffered or are suffering for the faith, we may well say "What is all this to me?". The answer is very simple, it is "Everything!" for since God is Love we too must love, and love and suffering are so inextricably linked that suffering is bound to be the lot of all true Christian people.

The message of the Old Testament is that God sees the suffering of His faithful people, He has compassion (not simply pity) on them. He is their Rock, their Fortress, He helps them in their affliction, they may have trust and confidence in Him.

In the New Testament *Acts 7.vv54-60* we read of Stephen, the first martyr of the Christian era, not only facing martyrdom bravely but, like his Master Jesus Christ, forgiving his persecutors praying that they might be forgiven.

The Gospel reading *(John 16.vv.1-11)* shows Jesus predicting persecution and suffering for His followers. None could say "Lord, you might have warned us"; not once but many times Jesus foretold the sufferings His followers would experience - the glory could not be without the Cross. Jesus promised, however, that by His Holy Spirit He would be ever with them to guide, uphold, strengthen and comfort them. It is important to realise that the word "Comforter" used so often for the Holy Spirit is all too often too weak a word associated with a "soothing hand" rather than the robust and powerful force implicit in the word comfort, for comfort is an intensive form of "fort" (cf fortress, fortitude) a strong and strengthening factor.

The rushing mighty wind of Pentecost, the flame and wind that swept away all doubts and fears are all attributes of God's mighty power and help.

Christian people know how much they need the power and protection of God's Spirit and if anyone should imagine that he or she could succeed without it they are mistaken. So too those who imagine that they can be loyal and steadfast witnesses to the faith without suffering should think again, for all who love inevitably suffer.

All Christian people are faced by enemies without and within. From within, if we are to follow Christ we must fight the forces of pride, jealousy, hatred, love of self comfort, greed, lethargy, impurity, acquiescence in evil.

From without, we witness in a hostile environment pressures to conform to the standards and norms of a "naughty" world where honesty, purity, compassion, love are often set at naught.

The dangers we face are more subtle than outright persecution but every bit as real and involve us in suffering, if not in persecution.

Jesus predicted suffering for His people even as He suffered on the Cross but "Lo, I am with you always even to the end of the world", said He, Thanks be to God.

A8   MARRIAGE

St. Mark 10.vv.2-16

~ Some Pharisees came, and to test Jesus they asked, "Is it lawful for a man to divorce his wife?". He answered them, "What did Moses command you?". They said, "Moses allowed a man to write a certificate of dismissal and to divorce her". But Jesus said to them, "Because of your hardness of heart he wrote this commandment for you. But from the beginning of creation, "God made them male and female". For this reason a man shall leave his father and mother and be joined to his wife, and the two shall become one flesh. So they are no longer two but one flesh. Therefore what God has joined together let no one separate".

Then in the house the disciples asked him again about this matter. He said to them, "Whoever divorces his wife and marries another commits adultery against her; and if she divorces her husband and marries another she commits adultery".

People were bringing little children to him in order that he might touch them; and the disciples spoke sternly to them. But when Jesus saw this, he was indignant and said to them, "Let the little children come to me; do not stop them; for it is to such as these that the kingdom of God belongs. Truly I tell you, whoever does not receive the kingdom of God as a little child will never enter it." And he took them up in his arms, laid his hands on them, and blessed them. ~

In an age when the family and the marriage bond are in such danger of being broken by the forces of Antichrist and the secular world, it is good to look back at the roots of our Christian faith so that we may be strengthened to press on in loyalty and love.

Among the many joys of being an ordained minister in the Church is that from time to time one has the privilege and joy of conducting marriages in Church.

The marriage service begins with a lengthy introduction setting out the purpose and nature of marriage and declaring God's purposes for family life.

In an early paragraph we read "In marriage husband and wife belong to one another". I have witnessed elderly couples saying to one another, "You belong to me and I belong to you". What a wonderful affirmation of love and loyalty! This is a fulfilment of Christ's teaching taken from the Old Testament that a man shall leave his father and mother ... cleave to his wife ... so they shall become one flesh. "What God has joined - let no man put asunder". The symbolic joining of hands, the giving of promises and of (a) ring(s) seal the convenant made before God.

A little later in the introduction we read, "husband and wife begin a new life together". The tragedy all too often is that marriage is for some people only a continuation of what has gone before. There is no zest for new ways of thinking and being in their relationship together or in the community. All too many couples think that marriage is an end not a beginning and fail to realise that a marriage is something to be worked at throughout one's earthly life.

In *Proverbs 31.vv.10-end* from the Old Testament, we have a lovely passage describing the good wife, her love, loyalty, prudence, care, concern and love for her husband and family.

The New Testament reading *(Ephesians 5vv.25-26)* bids husbands "love" their wives (not eros or philia, but "agape" is the word the writer uses), that love which is self-renunciating, sacrificial, actively seeking the good of others (did not Jesus command His followers to love (agape) one another?). This love is an understanding, forgiving love which gives and accepts pardon. The writer bids parents be forbearing with their children not driving them to resentment, but disciplining them in love.

In the Gospel reading after stressing the permanence of the marriage bond, Jesus *(Mark 10.vv.2-16)* speaks of the value of children in the family and in God's sight.

There is a strange Old Testament proverb in Ecclesiastes (the book so seldom read) that has a message for the newly-weds in a Church marriage: "A threefold cord is not easily broken". One cord may be snapped if one has strong fingers, but intertwined with a second is very strong. If a third cord is woven into these, scarcely can it be broken. In marriage, cord one is Bill's love for Jane, cord two is Jane's love for Bill, but cord three is the love that God has for Bill and Jane (the one flesh).

In marriages there will always be disagreements, open or tacit. There may be frustration, disappointment, anger and sorrow. Then is the time to realise that the God who shares our joys also shares our sorrows, that he is there to show compassion and forgiveness, to bring reconciliation, to restore harmony and joy to the marriage relationship. Thanks be to God.

"Bind us together, Lord, bind us together, in bonds that cannot be broken" we sing.

A9 ANYIETY

St. Matthew 6.vv.24-34

~ Jesus said, "No one can serve two masters; for a slave will either hate the one and love the other, or be devoted to one and despise the other. You cannot serve God and wealth. Therefore I tell you, do not worry about your life, what you will eat or what you will drink, or about your body, what you will wear. Is not life more than food, and the body more than clothing? Look at the birds of the air; they neither sow nor reap nor gather into barns, yet your heavenly Father feeds them. Are you not of more value than they? And can any of you by worrying add a single hour to your span of life? And why do you worry about clothing? Consider the lilies of the field, how they grow; they neither toil nor spin, Yet I tell you, even Solomon in all his glory was not clothed like one of them. But if God so clothes the grass of the field, which is alive today and tomorrow is thrown into the oven, will he not much more clothe you - you of little faith? Therefore do not worry, saying, "What will we eat" or "What will we drink?" or "What will we wear?". For it is the Gentiles who strive for all these things; and indeed your heavenly Father knows that you need all these things. But strive first for the kingdom of God and his righteousness, and all these things will be given to you as well.

So do not worry about tomorrow, for tomorrow will bring worries of its own. Today's trouble is enough for today". ~

One of the most poignant and tragic incidents brought to my notice is the true account of one who on his death bed recalled that the things that had given him most anxiety were the things that had never happened.

Among the manifold causes of physical, mental and spiritual dis-ease, anxiety is paramount.

75

Psychiatrists have asserted, probably with good reason, that a very large number of beds in General as well as Psychiatric Hospitals are occupied by people with no organic or physical ills but only anxiety-related ills.

Modern medicine supports such contentions; and experiences of the individual confirm that in times of stress and anxiety the physical body is far more prone to suffer the invasion of infectious diseases, aches and pains.

Many books and treatises have been written on the subject of healing but the majority concentrate on the holistic approach, i.e. of the whole person. How often it is proved necessary to allay fears and to reassure the sick before healing can take place. The Christian Church has naturally followed the example of Jesus in attempting to drive out guilt feelings as a precondition of healing. The classical example of healing through sin forgiven is to be found in *Mark 2.vv.1-12.*

One of the foremost Christian Psychiatrists of our day is the Swiss Paul Tournier whose books, written in a scholarly yet popular vein, exemplify the power of a mind at peace to bring healing to the body. Compared with what we might term the "secular healer", the "Christian healer" has the great advantage that he or she can give the assurance of sin forgiven in the name of Him from whom alone all healing comes.

It is perhaps unfortunate that the terms "healing" and "healer" are so often applied in reference to human efforts in medicine and surgery. What the medical, nursing and caring agencies are doing is to provide the means whereby healing can be facilitated or made possible for God - He alone heals - we simply co-operate with Him.

Perhaps even more tragic than the mind ill at ease or anxiety-ridden is the refusal or inability of so many sufferers (even sincere Christians) to accept the knowledge that in Christ all sin can be forgiven. It is as though, accepting intellectually that God has put the sin "behind his back" we* try to drag it out again and make ourselves miserable or anxious by dwelling on it again.

* the shift to the first person plural is not without significance.

A10 "GIVE ME"

St. Matthew 14.vv.1-2

~ At that time Herod the ruler heard reports about Jesus; and he said to his servants, "This is John the Baptist; he has been raised from the dead, and for

this reason these powers are at work in him". For Herod had arrested John, bound him, and put him in prison on account of Herodias, his brother Philip's wife, because John had been telling him, "It is not lawful for you to have her". Though Herod wanted to put him to death, he feared the crowd, because they regarded him as a prophet. But when Herod's birthday came, the daughter of Herodias danced before the company, and she pleased Herod so much that he promised on oath to grant her whatever she might ask. Prompted by her mother, she said, "Give me the head of John the Baptist here on a platter". The king was grieved, yet out of regard for his oaths and for the guests, he commanded it to be given; he sent and had John beheaded in prison. The head was brought on a platter and given to the girl, who brought it to her mother. His disciples came and took the body and buried it; then they went and told Jesus. ~

Fairy stories often have the theme "Ask for what you will and you shall have it", or "I grant you just one wish"; but here we are dealing not with a fairy story but a very grim story of folly, spite and cruelty.

In the Old Testament we read of Solomon in a dream being offered a free gift from God at the beginning of the kingship, "Ask what I shall give you". What a moment! What an opportunity for self aggrandisement! But no - he chose the gift of wisdom to govern aright God's people. Is it any wonder that the Lord was pleased with his modest request? The "wisdom" he was given may have been a kind of judicial astuteness and his later career may have belied his humility and sincerity, but nevertheless it was a very auspicious and commendable beginning to his career *(IKings 3.vv.4-15)*.

In the New Testament Herod Antipas's foolish promise to Salome : "Ask what you will up to half of my kingdom", brought upon him appalling shame and infamy - how awful! Poor John Baptist! He paid dearly for his courage and forthrightness; our Lord paid him a wonderful tribute :- "Of those that are born of women there has not arisen a greater than John the Baptist".

(Matthew 11.v11)

Jesus said "Ask and it shall be given you". Is this true? How often we hear, "Well, you jolly well asked for it!". Do we always ask for the right things, and are we sometimes denied those things we honestly believe are right to ask for? The answer to these questions is simply as Jesus taught us, "Thy will be done".

Like Solomon we are called, everyone of us, to a task of high destiny, nothing less than to represent Christ in the world. (He has no hands or feet or voice but ours). What then are we to ask for? Surely for the grace that brings us courage, Patience and Faith?

Courage - We crave for peace, but in our folly and the wisdom of God we are denied total peace. We can't avoid the clamour, the cries of pain, our involvement with the world. We can't slip out of the world, stop the world and get off; but we see the example of Jesus unflinching, never swamped by trouble or misfortune. He followed the way of the Cross, knowing that God was in control - the Lord was his strength and shield.

Patience - Is there anyone who does not fret, have bouts of ill-temper, chafe under the pettiness of man, grow moody or morose? We need to look to Jesus, bearing with the sin and folly of mankind. God is patient - "Wait then on God".

Faith - This means going on in the dark with Christ, trusting in God's loving purposes for his children. "Only believe", said Jesus to Jairus *(Mark 5.v36)*. Let us go on in faith, have courage and practise patience.

A11 COMPASSION

St. Luke 10.vv.25-37

~ *A lawyer stood up to test Jesus. "Teacher", he said, "What must I do to inherit eternal life?". He said to him, "What is written in the law? What do you read there?". He answered, "You shall love the Lord your God with all your heart, and with all your soul, and with all your strength, and with all your mind; and your neighbour as yourself." And he said to him, "You have given the right answer; do this and you will live".*

But wanting to justify himself he asked Jesus, "And who is my neighbour?". Jesus replied, "A man was going down from Jerusalem to Jericho, and fell into the hands of robbers, who stripped him, beat him, and went away, leaving him half dead. Now by chance a priest was going down that road; and when he saw him, he passed by on the other side. So likewise a Levite, when he came to the place and saw him, passed by on the other side. But a Samaritan while travelling came near him; and when he saw him, he was moved with pity. He went to him and bandaged his wounds having poured wine and oil on them. Then he put him on his own animal, brought him to an inn, and took care of him. The next day he took out two denarii, gave them to the innkeeper, and said, "Take care of him; and when I come back, I will repay you whatever more you spend". Which of these three, do you think, was a neighbour to the man who fell into the hands of robbers?". He said, "The one who showed him mercy". Jesus said to him, "Go and do likewise". ~

So vivid are Jesus' parables that it is hardly surprising to see on the roadside between Jerusalem and Jericho a "khan" (Inn) of the Samaritan. Standing alone outside the ruins during the 1939 - 1945 war, I realised also how vulnerable a traveller would be to a would-be mugger in that desolate terrain.

The teaching of this parable is so plain that we need constantly to remember the significance of the words "compassion" and "neighbour".

The Samaritan showed compassion. He did not merely have pity on the wounded man; probably the previous passers by pitied him too, for we can feel pity and look on from above, but compassion comes "where he is" and takes action. Compassion is a glorious word. In its original Greek, the word "compassion" denotes the movement of the bodily organs, "bowels" in some versions, "heart" in most. Compassion, as the word implies, means "suffer with", "come alongside"; today we more often use the word "empathise". Compassion is a Godlike quality; if God stopped short at pitying us, where should we be? All too often those who read or hear this parable wrongly assume that there was a tolerably good relationship and neighbourliness between the Samaritan and the wounded man. The Old Testament teaches concern and compassion for the neighbour. In Deuteronomy we read, "Leave some corn and grapes after harvest for your needy neighbour", a lovely idea. "Do not steal from, cheat or oppress your neighbour, love your neighbour as yourself". This is all very praiseworthy - but there is here a limited liability for the neighbour who is a Jew not a foreigner and certainly not an enemy.

In the New Testament St. Paul bids his hearers to show concern for one's enemies; bless them, don't curse them, overcome evil with good. How does this arise, that love is to be shown in this indiscriminate manner? The answer is simply that St. Paul has imbibed the teaching of Jesus Christ and followed his example, for the Jew and the Samaritan were not neighbours except in a territorial sense; the Jews were expected to despise or even hate the alien race of Samaritans; no love was lost between the two communities. Jesus, however, had an all-inclusive compassion for mankind. For Jesus there were no bounds; even "outcasts" were acceptable. "He came where we are" in the Incarnation. He died for all. By his cross he heals the hurts of all mankind and gives life by his death.

The message for us is plain - all too many are "half-dead", there is appalling human need, the "Jericho" road is everywhere. Sooner or later we find ourselves confronted by wounded brothers or sisters, wounded in body or spirit, and then we hear Jesus say, "Go thou, and do likewise".

A12 "IF ONLY"

St. Luke 19.vv.41-48

~ As Jesus came near and saw the city, he wept over it, saying, "If you, even you, had only recognised on this day the things that make for peace! But now they are hidden from your eyes. Indeed the days will come upon you, when your enemies will set up ramparts around you and surround you, and hem you in on every side. They will crush you to the ground, you and your children within you, and they will not leave within you one stone upon another; because you did not recognise the time of your visitation from God". Then he entered the temple and began to drive out those who were selling things there; and he said, "It is written, 'My house shall be a house of prayer', but you have made it a den of robbers". Every day he was teaching in the temple. The chief priests, the scribes and the leaders of the people kept looking for a way to kill him; but they did not find anything they could do, for all the people were spellbound by what they heard. ~

The two most tragic words in our, or any, language are "if" and "only" when joined together; "if only you knew" or "if only you had known" denote regret in hindsight or, in the context of this text, regret for that which is hidden from sight or knowledge.

Not on his own behalf, but for that of others, Jesus must often have repined or felt regret at the blindness, obtuseness, ignorance and failure of those he came to redeem.

Life for us all is full of frustration and disappointments; we all say, "If only I had known or realised ...".

The Gospel story of the five wise and five foolish girls *(Matthew 25.vv.1-13)* is a good example of the folly of being unprepared. The marriage customs described in the story may be unfamiliar, but the lesson is easily understood - "if only we had ...".

Many people have recurring dreams by night of lost opportunities, lost things, lost places. Psychologists recognise that beginning with infantile frustration and sense of loss we may be haunted by feelings of loss throughout our lives unless by God's grace we recover that which we have lost. But how, it may be objected, can we do this?

The answer is simply <u>we</u> cannot, but <u>God</u> can. If we have "lost our way" in life, full of regret and penitence we have the Good News of the Gospel - God

80

desires to love and care for us; we have the presence of Christ with us; God forgives and offers us another chance. We may have lost our ideals and fallen short of the glory of God, but Christ can raise us up. We may have lost our joy in life, but he who spoke of his joy and peace as he went to the Cross can restore our joy. What many of us regret most is the lost opportunity - "if only I had ... if only I had not ... said or done ...". Some things cannot be unsaid or undone, but the Good News is that God forgives and Christ never casts us off. Christianity is not simply the religion of the "Second Chance". A cat has only nine lives, we say, but by God's grace we have again and again the chance to repent (turn round) and begin again in the power and grace of the Lord Jesus.

A13 **PRAYER**

St. John 17.vv.11b-19

~ Jesus said, "I am coming to you. Holy Father, protect them in your name that you have given me, so that they may be one as we are one. While I was with them, I protected them in your name that you have given me. I guarded them and not one of them was lost except the one destined to be lost, so that the scripture might be fulfilled. But now I am coming to you, and I speak these things in the world so that they may have my joy made complete in themselves. I have given them your word, and the world has hated them because they do not belong to the world, just as I do not belong to the world. I am not asking you to take them out of the world, but I ask you to protect them from the evil one. They do not belong to the world, just as I do not belong to the world. Sanctify them in truth, your word is truth. As you have sent me into the world, so I have sent them into the world. And for their sakes I sanctify myself, so that they also may be sanctified in truth". ~

What a privilege it is for us to have such examples of Jesus' practice and teaching about prayer! For him it might truly be said that his whole life consisted of prayer, because he was ever mindful of the close presence of the Father which is the pre-condition and absolute requirement of all valid praying - nevertheless there were numerous occasions when he retired into solitude away from the world in order to realise more fully the presence of God and to listen to what God had to say to him.

Isaiah in the Old Testament knew something of this. "Be still and know that I am God". Samuel was taught, "Speak, Lord, for thy servant heareth". Here are two prerequisites of prayer that we often ignore to our hurt.

Silent contemplation and adoration must be the first step in meaningful prayer. Having assured ourselves of God's presence in our praying, we should next try to establish a right relationship with him, which involves confession of our sins and our unworthiness and asking his grace and pardon for all the hurt which we have inflicted upon God and our fellows. When we have truly repented and received pardon and peace, our hearts should be filled with gratitude and a desire to say thank you to God for this and all other benefits that he has bestowed upon us.

Jesus, teaching his disciples to pray, bade them give thanks for all the blessings of the past, for all their present mercies and for all their hopes for the future. Acknowledging our utter dependence upon God we thank him for all his goodness and loving kindness to us, and then, and only then, do we come to the point of laying before God our desires for ourselves, those we love and for all mankind.

In our reading from St. John's Gospel, we "overhear" Jesus praying for others, for us, for all God's children. There come times in the lives of us all when prayers of supplication for ourselves and intercession for others become difficult to sustain". "Ora pro nobis" (Pray for us) is a heartfelt prayer we often raise, and we know that the praying Church, our family and friends are continually "lifting us up" in prayer when we are weak in body, mind or spirit.

Jesus taught us to "make our requests known to God". There is nothing that we should hold back out of mock modesty, timidity or faithlessness - provided only that we pray as Jesus did in the faith that God, who knows us and our needs better than we do, will grant us what is best for us and for those for whom we pray.

Occasionally we are privileged to "overhear", as it were, the words Jesus addressed to the Father in prayer, but more often it was a wordless and loving converse with God as it is with so many who know God's presence in their lives, as in the case of old "Jacques", a saintly peasant who every day spent time alone in the village Church. On being asked, "What do you say or do in the Church?", he replied, "He just looks at me, and I just looks (sic) at Him".

In prayer , the ways and the postures we adopt, the words we use, are myriad. Jesus, as a Jew was heir to a tradition in which the arms and eyes were raised to heaven and a "free and frank discussion" took place with the Almighty. Those who have seen the "Fiddler on the Roof" appreciate the frankness so often seen in the Psalms when God is urged to "bestir himself" and come to the aid of his people - such candour is no doubt acceptable to God, for to whom else can one complain? Jesus is continually represented to us as praying long and earnestly (his whole life a life of prayer).

A14 DEATH

St. John 11.vv.17-27

~ *When Jesus arrived, he found that Lazarus had already been in the tomb four days. Now Bethany was near Jerusalem, some two miles away, and many of the Jews had come to Martha and Mary to console them about their brother. When Martha heard that Jesus was coming, she went and met him, while Mary stayed at home. Martha said to Jesus, "Lord, if you had been here, my brother would not have died. But even now I know that God will give you whatever you ask of him". Jesus said to her, "Your brother will rise again". Martha said to him, "I know that he will rise again in the resurrection on the last day". Jesus said to her, "I am the resurrection and the life. Those who believe in me, even though they die, will live, and everyone who lives and believes in me will never die. Do you believe this?". She said to him, "Yes, Lord, I believe that you are the Messiah, the Son of God, the one coming into the world". ~*

It has been stated with a fair degree of reason that in the Victorian Era death was overtly contemplated physically and figuratively, and sex was hidden away, but that in the 20th century the position has been completely reversed.

Certainly sex has been flaunted and death "played down" in recent years. It does not follow that death has been trivialised. On the contrary, with the weakening of Christian beliefs about eternal life and the gross ignorance of many about Christian teaching concerning death, a mystique and sometimes fear and despair have arisen when the subject is broached.

In previous generations, especially when infant mortality was higher and extended families were the rule, even young children became habituated to the visitation of death to the home and the spectacle of their loves ones deceased.

Today, unless requested to the contrary, Undertakers are expected to remove the deceased post- haste from the home and to keep the bodies in a "chapel of rest". Seldom do relatives ask to see their dead.

As a priest involved in many funeral visits and ceremonies, I have, nevertheless, been impressed by the number of people who, though they never "darken the Church door", yet have a profound regard for the ministrations of the Church in times of mourning and are even brought back to the Christian faith through the experience of losing a loved one. It is seldom that one ever encounters anything but a deep reverence for life and death and a desire to fathom these mysteries.

One of the most intractable problems that I have ever encountered in the homes of death is in reassuring the living that the sense of guilt and remorse towards the deceased is one that we all share and which we need to work through. Knowing how we all hurt and neglect those we love most, and how we suffer the pangs of guilt, we do well to remember that such feelings can only be truly assuaged by (sometimes open) confession and by the grace and comfort of God into whose hands we commend our loved ones, and who alone can forgive our sins.

A15 HYPOCRISY

St. Mark 7.vv.1-23

~ Now when the Pharisees and some of the scribes who had come from Jerusalem gathered around Jesus, they noticed that some of his disciples were eating with defiled hands, that is, without washing them. (For the Pharisees, and all the Jews, do not eat unless they thoroughly wash their hands, thus observing the tradition of the elders, and they do not eat anything from the market unless they wash it, and there are also many other traditions that they observe, the washing of cups, pots, and bronze kettles.) So the Pharisees and the scribes asked him, "Why do your disciples not live according to the tradition of the elders, but eat with defiled hands?". He said to them, "Isaiah prophesied rightly about you hypocrites, as it is written, 'This people honours me with their lips, but their hearts are far from me, in vain do they worship me, teaching human precepts as doctrines.' You abandon the commandment of God and hold to human tradition". Then he said to them, "You have a fine way of rejecting the commandment of God in order to keep your tradition! For Moses said, 'Honour your father and mother' and 'Whoever speaks evil of father or mother must surely die'. But you say that if anyone tells father or mother, 'Whatever support you might have from me is Corban' (that is an offering to God) - then you no longer permit doing anything for a father or mother, thus making void the word of God through your tradition that you have handed on. And you do many things like this".

Then he called the crowd again and said to them, "Listen to me, all of you and understand: there is nothing outside a person that by going in can defile, but the things that come our are what defile."

When he had left the crowd and entered the house, his disciples asked him about the parable. He said to them, "Then do you also fail to understand? Do you not see that whatever goes into a person from outside cannot defile, since it enters not the heart, but the stomach, and goes out into the sewer?". (Thus he declared all foods clean). And he said, "It is what comes out of a person that defiles. For it is from within, from the human heart, that evil intentions come; fornication, theft, murder, adultery, avarice, wickedness, deceit, licentiousness, envy, slander, pride, folly. All these evil things come from within, and they defile a person." ~

This reading is of tremendous importance because it shows how different were the views of Jesus from those of the Pharisees and Scribes on what constitutes true religion.

It foreshadows the Cross in demonstrating how hostile the religious authorities would be towards Jesus, his teachings and his acts.

It warns us against mistaking the trappings and legalism of religion for a genuine faith.

It centres upon the "tradition of the elders", a hide-bound, legalistic system that developed within Jewry, at the best providing helpful guidelines for conduct and spirituality but, unfortunately, at its worst having a strangling effect upon its most ardent practitioners.

The basic idea of this cultus was the concept of "Holiness", that is, "apartness"; there must be no contamination in religious or even secular affairs (and the dividing line, if any, was very thin!).

Jesus deals with several aspects of "contamination". First, he deals with Koinos, i.e. "common", that is unclean, unwashed hands. The many rules and regulations concerning this have little to do with hygiene, but a prescribed ritual making one acceptable to God. Jesus, though a Jew, would have none of it!

Next Jesus refers to cleanliness of vessels. Though apparently clean, vessels could be contaminated by "unclean" persons or foods. People could be "unclean", that is, taboo after child-bearing, by contact with death or with Gentiles and in various other ways - but Jesus, though a Jew, would have none of it!

The unfamiliar word "Corban" refers to dedicating objects to God's service whilst neglecting the pressing needs of even one's nearest and dearest. Jesus, though a Jew, would have none of it!

These are some of the practices to which Jesus was opposed. He spoke a different language! There is here a fundamental cleavage.

For the ultra-orthodox Jew as represented by the Scribes and Pharisees, religion consisted of ritual, regulations and ceremonial duly observed. For Jesus and his followers, religion was purely a matter of loving and serving God and one's fellows.

Jesus charged the Pharisees and Scribes with "hypocrisy". The word refers to play acting, that is, masking one's true identity, one's genuine self. There is a sense in which we all "put on a face" before the world. If we do this to encourage and help others, and also bare our souls before God - all well and good; but we should take to heart Jesus' strictures on the hypocrisy he witnessed and strive to ensure that our religion is pure and undefiled, a loving response to the love of God for what he has done for us.

A16 LIFTED UP

St. John 3.vv.13-21

~ No one has ascended into heaven except the one who descended from heaven, the Son of Man. And just as Moses lifted up the serpent in the wilderness, so must the Son of Man be lifted up, that whoever believes in him may have eternal life. For God so loved the world that he gave his only Son, so that everyone who believes in him may not perish but have eternal life. Indeed, God did not send the Son into the world to condemn the world, but in order that the world might be saved through him. Those who believe in him are not condemned; but those who do not believe are condemned already, because they have not believed in the name of the only Son of God. And this is the judgement that the light has come into the world, and people loved darkness rather than light because their deeds were evil. For all who do evil hate the light, so that their deeds may not be exposed. But those who do what is true come to the light, so that it may be clearly seen that their deeds have been done in God. ~

"As Moses lifted up the serpent in the wilderness, so must the Son of Man be lifted up, that whosoever believes in Him may have eternal life".

Whether or not these are the exact words of Jesus or whether they are the Evangelist's meditation upon Jesus' sacrificial death, we have here a fascinating insight into the significance of Jesus' life and death.

The reference to the "serpent" is most interesting. In the Old Testament we have a reference to the serpent as a cunning creature that tempts and leads mankind into rebellion and sin against God. Somewhat later in the Exodus account in which the making of graven images was strictly prohibited, we have the account referred to in this passage of the Israelites plagued by snake bites in the wilderness and gaining relief by gazing upon the representation of a serpent which Moses held aloft. Jewish Rabbis are at pains to stress that "it was not the serpent that gave life; but as long as it was uplifted, there was belief in him who commanded Moses to act thus" - it was <u>God</u> who healed. How right and sensible were these ancient Rabbis! It is interesting to note that the abhorrence of graven images persisted down through the years and King Hezekiah had a brazen image of "Nehushtan" the serpent destroyed during his religious reform programme. Nevertheless the association of the "healing serpent" persists in the medical profession's insignia.

St. John takes the lifting up of the serpent and applies it as a kind of parable to the "lifting up" of Jesus. As the ancient Jews looked at the serpent and their thoughts turned to God, they received healing; even so all who look up at Jesus will gain eternal life.

We may well wonder whether the lifting up of Jesus refers to the Cross or the Ascension but it hardly matters for the two are inextricably linked and the one could not have happened without the other. The Cross was the way to glory. Had Jesus not been crucified there would have been no glory. The same applies to us. If we choose the easy way, refusing the cross we are called to bear, we lose the glory - "No cross, no crown".

Gazing on Jesus is the first step to belief in God, for Jesus says, "He that hath seen me, has seen the Father". Jesus shows that God loves us, cares for us and wants nothing more than to forgive us. It was not easy for the ancient Jews to believe that, for was not God the one who imposed the Law, who punishes even the children of the sinner, the Judge before whom all are judged, the one who demanded sacrifices and burnt offerings? It took the life and cost the death of Jesus to tell mankind that things were otherwise.

As St. John says, the gift of Jesus is "eternal life". This eternal life leads to wholeness and peace. We gain peace with <u>God</u>; we feel at home with him; we are not estranged from him but reconciled to him. We gain peace with <u>other people</u>, for if we ourselves are forgiven we too can, and must, be forgiving. We gain peace with <u>life</u>, for God can, and wills to, work all things together for good, if we truly love him. We gain peace with <u>ourselves</u>, for we come to terms with our weakness through the grace and power of Christ indwelling us. We gain that peace which passes all understanding - a foretaste of that heaven to which we are called.

A17 GRACE AND TRUTH

St. John 1.vv.14-18

~ The word became flesh and lived among us, and we have seen his glory, the glory as of the father's only son, full of grace and truth. (John testified to him and cried out, "this was he of whom I said, he who comes after me ranks ahead of me because he was before me".). From his fullness we have all received grace upon grace. The law indeed was given through Moses; grace and truth came through Jesus Christ. No one has ever seen God. It is God the only Son who is close to the Father's heart, who has made him known. ~

"The law indeed was given by Moses; grace and truth came through Jesus Christ." *(John 1.v17)*

It is recorded that a Jewish Rabbi was once present at a banquet in America and seated next to a rather pompous woman who proudly declared, "One of my ancestors was present at the signing of the Declaration of Independence". "Really?", said the Rabbi, "One of my ancestors wrote the Ten Commandments".

It is not only the Jewish people who venerate the memory of Moses, "The Man of God". In many ancient Churches are found lists of the Ten Commandments inscribed in word or stone, such is the importance Christians also attach to them; for they are "The Maker's Instructions". The things that belong to our peace; laws which undergird the very fabric of social and religious life. Jesus as a Jew upheld and honoured the laws, "I am not come to destroy but to fulfil".

St. John in the prologue to his gospel declares that whereas Moses gave the law, through Jesus came grace and truth.

All too often our words are debased in current usage. This applies particularly to some of our most precious words; "love" for instance can be used of the highest and the lowest; love of fish and chips, our pets, our family, of God. The word is used indiscriminately in common speech, but fortunately the lovely word "grace" remains relatively unsullied.

There are two aspects (among others) that we see in grace; first, there is sheer beauty and winsomeness; even his enemies marvelled at the gracious words of Jesus and men, women and children were attracted by the warmth of his personality. Secondly, there is the unconditional, universal, sacrificial love of

Christ for the undeserving. None of us merits the love, compassion, restoration and reconciliation which Jesus offers to mankind. All is of "grace".

The word "truth" is used not only about Jesus, but by him when he said, "I am the Way, the Truth and the Life". Pilate asked "What is truth?" for he did not know or care to acknowledge that the one who stood before him on trial was the very personification of truth. Truth is not simply the opposite of lies and untruth. Truth is that which "sets us free", as Jesus declared, truth frees us from self and selfish desires, from the bondage of sin, of greed, of lust and all those things that destroy our peace. As the truth himself, Jesus teaches us the truth about God and about mankind and those things that belong to our peace.

A18 TALENTS

St. Matthew 25.vv.14-28

~ For it is as if a man, going on a journey, summoned his slaves and entrusted his property to them; to one he gave five talents, to another two, to another one, to each according to his ability. Then he went away. The one who had received the five talents went off at once and traded with them, and made five more talents. In the same way the one who had the two talents made two more talents. But the one who had received the one talent went off and dug a hole in the ground and hid his master's money. After a long time the master of those slaves came and settled accounts with them. Then the one who had received the five talents came forward bringing five more talents, saying, "Master, you handed over to me five talents; see, I have made five more talents". His master said to him, "Well done, good and trustworthy slave; you have been trustworthy in a few things, I will put you in charge of many things; enter into the joy of your master". And the one with the two talents also came forward, saying, "Master, you handed over to me two talents; see, I have made two more talents". His master said to him, "Well done, good and trustworthy slave; you have been trustworthy in a few things, I will put you in charge of many things; enter into the joy of your master". Then the one who had received the one talent also came forward, saying, "Master, I knew that you were a harsh man, reaping where you did not sow, and gathering where you did not scatter seed; so I was afraid, and went and hid your talent in the ground. Here you have what is yours". But his master replied, "You wicked and lazy slave! You knew, did you, that I reap where I did not sow, and gather where I did not scatter? Then you ought to have invested my money with the bankers, and on my return I would have received what was my own with interest". ~

Samuel Clements (Mark Twain) once said, "Other people are worried about the Bible passages they don't understand. As for me, it's the passages I do understand that worry me most"! But here is a parable we all understand, for the parable of the Talents is about responsibility before God for all he has given us.

In the parable the prudent owner of the estate entrusts his possessions to his servants in his absence, giving to each according to his ability, and one of them fails miserably in the task. Isn't that exactly what God does with us? He makes a wonderful world and gives it to us in trust and we have to get on with the running of it. St. Peter says, "Like good stewards of the manifold grace of God, serve one another with whatever gift each of you has received". What gifts we have received! The Holy Spirit is ever present as a guide and strengthener - yet what a mess we often make of this life!

Our gifts and abilities that we call talents are God-given, therefore God expects of us results commensurate with our abilities for our good, for the good of all his people and for his glory. But one might say, "Are not some born devoid of talents in the sense of abilities? What of the baby born mentally defective and physically handicapped? What is expected in such a case?". The answer must surely be that such a tragedy is contrary to the will of a loving heavenly Father, but the talent of such a one lies in the power to evoke compassion, love and service in those who care for and love that child.

It is true that we are not all born equal in ability, but we can be equal in our efforts to employ our gifts. God calls ordinary people to do extraordinary things in his service and as Abraham Lincoln once said, "God must love ordinary people, he made so many of them!".

If we do not use our talents there is a very grave danger that we shall lose them. How many of us through lack of practice have lost the ability to speak foreign languages or to play the piano? Some have perverted or abused their gifts as skilful burglars or assassins. We may simply ignore or neglect our talents or be afraid to venture as the good-for-nothing servant in the parable. As Christians we are continually being called to adventurous living, to venture in faith. We must not stagnate or be continually looking to the past. By all means let us look to and learn from the past, but we are being called to go forward. Christianity is a "Way" and we are "pilgrim people" on the way.

Do we measure our progress continually? Each time we come to Church do we leave at least a little more loving, accepting, patient and considerate?

A19 THE BAPTIST

St. Luke 7.vv.24-35

~ *When John's messengers had gone, Jesus began to speak to the crowds about John; "What did you go out into the wilderness to look at? A reed shaken by the wind? What then did you go out to see? Someone dressed in soft robes? Look, those who put on fine robes and live in luxury are in royal palaces. What then did you go out to see? A prophet? Yes, I tell you, and more than a prophet. This is one about whom it is written, 'See, I am sending my messenger ahead of you, who will prepare your way before you'. I tell you, among those born of women no one is greater than John; yet the least in the kingdom of God is greater than he." (And all the people who heard this, including the tax collectors, acknowledged the justice of God, because they had been baptised with John's baptism. But by refusing to be baptised by him the Pharisees and the lawyers rejected God's purpose for themselves.)*

"To what then will I compare the people of this generation, and what are they like? They are like children sitting in the marketplace and calling to one another. 'We played the flute for you, and you did not dance; we wailed, and you did not weep.' For John the Baptist has come eating no bread and drinking no wine, and you say, 'He has a demon'; the Son of Man has come eating and drinking, and you say, 'Look, a glutton and a drunkard, a friend of tax collectors and sinners!' Nevertheless, wisdom is vindicated by all her children." ~

If, as some have suggested, there was a tendency in the early Christian community for some people to exalt the person of John the Baptist at the expense of Jesus, it may well be due partly to the intrinsic character of John and partly to the tribute that Jesus paid him. "Of those that are born of woman, there has not appeared a greater than John the Baptist". Who would not accord honour and respect to one who displayed such courage and devotion as John - and yet, with true humility, continually pointed away from himself to Jesus?

The account of the death of John the Baptist, recorded in *Mark 6.vv.14-29*, is one of the most gruesome stories in the Gospel, apart from the account of Jesus' death. His imprisonment and death were directly caused by his outspoken condemnation of the behaviour of Herod Antipas who, together with Pilate *(Luke 23.vv.6-12)*, also shared responsibility for Jesus' death.

These similarities in the behaviour and beliefs of Jesus and John are, however, less striking than the identity of their message when each began his ministry. The keynote of their message was the word "REPENT".

It is a great pity that the word "repent" has such weak and negative connotations both in the Church and in the world outside. For countless thousands of people, repentance means simply "sorrow for sin", acknowledging one's wretchedness. Such ideas are truly involved in repentance, but this is only the first step in showing what the Greek word "metanoia" means. Greek words beginning with "meta" always involve change or something following on. "Noia" (nous) means "mind" so that when we think of metanoia we should be thinking of something positive, that is a change of mind, heart, spirit, lifestyle, spiritual life, a radical reassessment of our lives as individuals and subsequently, of course, of society.

This new quality of life is referred to in many ways in the New Testament. Jesus refers to "spiritual rebirth" in his talk with Nicodemus, and the Epistles stress continually the new life in the Spirit.

We know what is involved in "metanoia", but not everyone knows how this radical change can be effected in our lives. One thing is quite certain. As St. Paul says, "What I would not, I do; and what I would do, I do not. Wretched man that I am, who can rescue me from this body of death?" - and then there comes the triumphal shout, "Thanks be to God through Jesus Christ our Lord!". St. Paul knew as all Christians acknowledge that we cannot transform our lives or undergo a spiritual transformation by our own efforts. It is too much like "trying to pull ourselves up by our boot laces". There is only one way. Only Christ by the Holy Spirit can effect this change in our lives. He alone can transform and transfigure us.

Whenever I am called upon to baptise a little one in Church, I always ask myself (and sometimes the congregation) the question asked about the infant John the Baptist, *(Luke 1.v.66)*, "What then will this child be?". St. Luke adds, "The hand of the Lord was with him".

A20 STEWARDSHIP

St. Luke 12.vv.41-48

~ Peter said, "Lord, are you telling this parable for us or for everyone?" And the Lord said, "Who then is the faithful and prudent manager whom his master will put in charge of his slaves, to give them their allowance of food at the proper time? Blessed is that slave whom his master will find at work when he arrives. Truly I tell you, he will put that one in charge of all his possessions. But if that slave says to himself, 'My master is delayed in coming', and if he begins to beat the other slaves, men and women, and to eat and drink and get drunk, the master of that slave will come on a day when he does not expect him and at an hour that he does not know, and will cut him in

pieces, and put him with the unfaithful. That slave who knew what his master wanted, but did not prepare himself or do what was wanted, will receive a severe beating. But the one who did not know and did what deserved a beating will receive a light beating. From everyone to whom much has been given, much will be required, and from the one to whom much has been entrusted, even more will be demanded." ~

We all have our private or vocational nightmares. For me as a priest one is arriving too late for a Service which I should have conducted - "they've all gone home!".

On one occasion recently I was ready in good time to set off for a Church about 12 miles distant but my car wasn't, because the battery had discharged overnight. Feeling a rising panic, I knocked up a neighbour and asked him to lend me his car. He readily agreed since he was attending the local Church. I have never driven a car more carefully in my 60 years at the wheel. The car was older than mine, but it was not mine; if I had damaged it, I could never have forgiven myself. However, by lunch time I was safely back at his home to return the car with heartfelt relief.

I began later to reflect on what a responsibility we undertake when we use or share what does not belong to us. In so many ways we are guardians and stewards of what does not belong to us alone. I began to ask myself, does anything in this world really belong to me?

This is God's world. He is Creator and Redeemer. Of his grace and free will he gives us life and breath and all the blessings of this life. My house and the Church in which worship I cannot call my own. Others, like me, shared them before me, and hopefully others will after me. "Naked I came from my mother's womb and naked shall I return" said Job. "You can't take it with you", are words often addressed to those who would cling to earthly possessions, for they are not ours. We hold them in trust from God, but how we make use of them while they are in our keeping is a very serious matter. Even our nearest and dearest we cannot hold back when God calls them to himself. "All souls are thine, dear Lord, who gavest them to us, yet as thou didst not lose them in the giving, even so we do not lose them on their departing from us", said John Donne. Our Christian hope and trust is that those whom we have loved and lost we shall meet again in God's eternal kingdom - but the loss is sad and severe at parting. How important it is therefore to appreciate, cherish and preserve those people and things that God has given us. Wise stewardship is one of those important lessons that Jesus teaches us in the Gospels. We must be ready to give back to God all that we say we own.

One of God's greatest gifts to us is time, yet we often hear people say "I'm sorry but I have no time" (even to pray!). What they really mean is "I have all the time in the world (as we all have), but I have not organised my life, my priorities aright. Truly we live under pressures today; but the problem is not lack of time but control of it. Jesus died young, but the quality of his short life far surpassed that of those of us who have grown old. What he attempted, by God's grace he achieved.

In Church we make our offerings giving back to God what he has first given to us. "All things come of thee", we say, "and of thine own do we give thee". Jesus had much to say about the poor and the rich, about generosity and covetousness. Some of his most stringent teaching concerned the love of riches. What we give to his service is a measure of our love and what he means to us. Someone once asked, "When do we know when to stop giving?". The answer is simply, "Stop, when the Saviour stops giving to you".

A21 SALT

St. Matthew 5.vv.13-16

~ *"You are the salt of the earth; but if salt has lost its taste, how can its saltiness be restored? It is no longer good for anything, but is thrown out and trampled under foot. You are the light of the world. A city built on a hill cannot be hid. No one after lighting a lamp puts it under the bushel basket, but on the lampstand and it gives light to all the house. In the same way, let your light shine before others, so that they may see your good works and give glory to your Father in heaven".* ~

To be called 'the salt of the earth' is a compliment. In ancient days salt was described as "theion", that is "divine". Why, one might wonder, was it accorded such value? The answer is that it had such important properties. Jesus said his disciples were the salt of the earth. The qualities that he had in mind were those of his contemporaries to whom salt was a most important commodity.

First salt denoted PURITY : Its glistening whiteness appealed to the ancients; the sacrifices of Israel were always offered with salt. Nowadays there is such a lowering of standards in social, political and economic life, through ignorance and wickedness. Honesty, diligence and high standards of morality are in some instances looked upon as outmoded values. Christians, however, are bidden to be pure in thought, word and deed. We should never compromise with impurity. Christians should protest against "smut" and blasphemy in the written word and upon the TV screen. We cannot opt out of the world, but we can keep ourselves unstained by the world. We can and must uphold the standards of purity.

Secondly salt is a PRESERVATIVE : In the days before the use of freezers and fridges, salt was used as the main preservative for food. Christians should have an antiseptic influence on life, preserving values and standards, cleansing, defeating corruption, helping others to be good, speaking out against evil, upholding good causes and never holding our peace out of fear or favour.

Thirdly salt gives FLAVOUR : Many foods are bland and tasteless without the addition of salt. Life for many is an insipid affair. Christianity should be to life as salt is to food. The tragedy is that all too often Christianity is associated with kill-joy experiences. The world may be bored and weary, but we should ever strive to discover lost radiance and the sparkle of true faith, for the Christian is the only person who has any right to hold an optimistic outlook on life, if we believe and trust in God's goodness and his sovereign power to bring success out of failure and joy out of sorrow.

It is unlikely that any day passes when we do not place the salt upon the table. If we believe the words of Jesus, each time we do this it could well be an opportunity to remind ourselves of what he expects and hopes of us

A similar action in everyday life could well remind us that we are called to be lights in the world. Jews both ancient and modern, following the practices of their forebears, touch the "mezuzah" on the doorposts of their homes as they enter or leave their homes. This little cylinder, containing a tiny portion of the Law, serves not as a piece of magic but as an aid to memory ("the Lord bless you in your going out and in your coming in"). Even so, we might in switching on and off our lights remind ourselves that having received the light of Christ we are bidden to shine as lights in the world to the glory of God.

A22 RECONCILIATION

St. John 17.vv.20-26

~ *"I ask not only on behalf of these, but also on behalf of those who will believe in me through their word, that they may all be one. As you, Father, are in me and I am in you, may they also be in us, so that the world may believe that you have sent me. The glory that you have given me I have given them, so that they may be one, as we are one. I in them and you in me, that they may become completely one, so that the world may know that you have sent me and have loved them even as you have loved me. Father, I desire that those also whom you have given me, may be with me where I am, to see my glory, which you have given me because you loved me before the foundation of the world. Righteous Father, the world does not know you, but I know you; and these know that you have sent me. I made your name known to them, and I will make it known so that the love with which you have loved me may be in them, and I in them."* ~

In 1945 in the awful aftermath of World War 2, when nations and people were torn apart and old hatreds were re-emerging, the Germans in penitence and reparation built for the Taize Community an enormous Church in France, dedicated to "reconciliation". It still bears the name of the "Church of Reconciliation"; so great is the need of reconciliation in the world today.

Nearly 50 years later in the former Yugoslavia we see similar tragedy, pain and need, a people torn asunder. We see harrowing pictures of wrecked towns, economies and lives; personal relationships have been shattered by "ethnic cleansing"; former neighbours and friends are alienated; thousands of people have been made homeless and refugees; thousands more injured or bereaved. What a task for would-be reconcilers!

Nearer at home we see broken relationships, homelessness often resulting from rejection, families torn apart by divorce.

St. Paul says, "God has entrusted us with the message of reconciliation. We come therefore as Christ's ambassadors". What a daunting task! If we are to be ambassadors, how shall we mediate and reconcile? Only by showing pardon and peace. But the problem is that we cannot mediate pardon and peace unless we know it in our <u>own</u> lives. There is nothing more tragic than trying to give what we have not got in the first place; this is a well known failure in unsuccessful counselling. How many of us have <u>not</u> gained pardon and peace! First of all we must be reconciled to ourselves. Many lives are filled with self-loathing, unquiet thoughts, guilty consciences and unresolved personal problems, so that we become poor ambassadors for this task. Unless we can gain pardon and peace for words that can't be unsaid, deeds that can't be undone, relationships that have not been mended, we cannot become Christ's ambassadors. What then are we to do?

Only by being put right with God can we gain pardon and peace. In his great letter to the Romans Paul tells us that we can be reconciled or put right with God by faith, by repentance and by accepting the proffered love of God. Here we find our pardon and peace with God and ourselves, and thus become mediators and ministers of reconciliation in the world.

The trouble is that so often we prefer to struggle on beneath a burden of sin that we could lay down at the foot of the cross of Christ. Consider John

Bunyan's account in "Pilgrim's Progress" of how Christian was loosed from his burden of sin and gained pardon, peace and joy. "Now I saw in my dream that Christian toiled with difficulty up the hill by reason of the heavy burden that he carried on his back, but at the top of the hill there stood a cross. At the foot of this cross Christian knelt, whereupon the burden was loosed from his back and rolled back down the hill and fell into an empty tomb and he saw it no more. Then was Christian glad and lightsome and said with a merry heart, 'He hath given me rest by His sorrow, and life by his death'."

A23 DISCIPLESHIP

St. John 13.vv.31-35

~ *When Judas had gone out, Jesus said, "Now is the Son of Man glorified, and God has been glorified in him. If God has been glorified in him, God will also glorify him in himself and will glorify him at once. Little children, I am with you only a little longer. You will look for me; and as I said to the Jews so now I say to you, 'Where I am going you cannot come'. I give you a new commandment that you love one another. Just as I have loved you, you also should love one another. By this everyone will know that you are my disciples, if you have love for one another."* ~

Our reading speaks of something absolutely up to date and understood by all whether young or old, namely advertising. This is surely the great age of advertising, of trying to convince people that they need or want goods or services. Some advertisements are very amusing, some unintelligible, some pathetically poor, but they are all directed to the same end. In recent years we have seen a "rash" of T-shirts - some slightly obscene, some meaningless drawing attention to the self. There are thankfully some more honest and acceptable which draw attention to the dearly held beliefs of those who display them. Of such the "Ichthus" or fish symbol is a good example for it points to the one who is "Jesus Christ, Son of God, Saviour", using the initial letters of the Greek word for "fish", in itself a symbol of early Christianity.

But even if we do not seek to advertise ourselves or our beliefs or wish to draw others' attention to ourselves, we are nevertheless "public figures". "Smile, you're on TV" is the message of monitoring security cameras!

We may desire privacy but it is denied us. We are public spectacles, and what unprepossessing ones we sometimes are!

For Christians, as St. Paul says, there is a terrible terrifying responsibility for we advertise Christ. He does not say this in so many words, but if he were here (and is he not?) I am sure he would agree that is what he meant when he said, "We proclaim not ourselves but we proclaim Christ Jesus", and this we do by the quality of our lives - or like a cracked or distorting mirror we reflect a distorted reflection of Christ.

Do we in fact show in our lives that love, joy, and peace come from discipleship - for Our Lord said, "By this shall all people know you are my disciples if you have love for one another". Jesus did <u>not</u> say, "People will know you by what you say - but by what you <u>are</u>".

"Actions", we say, "speak louder than words". Of the early Christians it was said, "See how these Christians love one another". Visiting many Churches in my travels I can testify to the warmth and love of Christian congregations among whom the Holy Spirit works.

But we may well ask, "What is the nature of this love?". Jesus says he "commands" it! It cannot, therefore, be a love based solely upon a sentiment or feeling; it cannot be loving because the loved one is attractive and lovable; or the mutual regard of those who have "fallen in love". A love commanded is a matter more of the will than the heart, a love that shows unconquerable good will to all mankind - the unloving, unlovable and unloved. It must be the disciplined love that persists in the face of rejection and hatred; if need be a love like that of Jesus who said "Father, forgive them" at the Cross, the love that cannot be defeated, the love of Christ for all sinful humanity loving the sinner whilst hating the sin. Jesus said, "If you love like this, all will know you are my disciples".

If indeed we love like this, the world will see in us the distinguishing marks of the true Christian radiance, joy and glory - those marks that non-Christians will recognise and by God's grace wistfully yearn after with a desire to be drawn into the Kingdom of God.

A24 LABOURERS

St. Matthew 20.vv.1-16

~ *The kingdom of heaven is like a landowner who went out early in the morning to hire labourers for his vineyard. After agreeing with the labourers for the usual daily wage, he sent them into his vineyard. When he went out about nine o'clock he saw others standing there idle in the marketplace; and he said to them, "You also go into the vineyard, and I will pay you whatever is right". So they went. When he went out about noon and about three o'clock, he did the same. And about five o'clock he went out and found others standing around; and he said to them, 'Why are you standing here idle all day?'. They said to him, 'Because no one has hired us'. He said to them, 'You also go into the vineyard'. When evening came, the owner of the vineyard said to his manager, 'Call the labourers and give them their pay, beginning with the last and then going to the first. When those hired about five o'clock came, each of them received the usual wage. Now when the first came, they thought they would receive more; but each of them also received the usual daily wage. And when they received it they grumbled against the landowner, saying, 'The last worked only one hour, and you have made them equal to us who have borne the burden of the day and the scorching heat'. But he replied, to one of them, 'Friend, I am doing you no wrong; did you not agree with me for the usual daily wage? Take what belongs to you and go; I choose to give to this last the same as I give to you. Am I not allowed to do what I choose with what belongs to me? Or are you envious because I am generous?'. So the last will be first, and the first will be last."* ~

Among all the parables of Jesus, one of my favourites is that of the 'Labourers in the Vineyard' yet whenever it is read publicly I always imagine I hear the spoken or unspoken criticism, "T'ain't fair!". Why should the last hired receive pay equal to the first? But I also think I hear Jesus say, "Why, bless you, of course it isn't, but that's not the point".

We are not concerned here with blueprints for industrial relations, strict justice, sound economies or anything of the sort - least of all a TUC practical policy! No, we are not concerned with how <u>employers</u> should act but how God <u>does</u> act.

Now ask yourself, "Do you really want to receive your due from God?". I certainly do not!

If we are to appreciate and understand this parable aright, we must consider carefully the details of it.

In Palestine the grape harvest was at the end of September, before the heavy rains came and produced a panic in gathering the harvest - even an hour's work could stave off crop ruination so that for the vineyard owner adequate casual labour was critical.

As in this country in days gone by, there were 'hiring days' and the marketplace became a 'labour exchange'. In the precarious economy of Palestine even one hour's work could stave off starvation for a labourer's family, so that we can see how important is the issue for the owner and his servants if their needs are to be satisfied - it could be a matter of life and death.

It is against this background that we must consider the fairness or otherwise of this splendid parable, which contains truths at the very heart of the Christian religion.

First, we consider the relief and comfort of those who obey Christ's injunction, "Come unto me all ye that are heavy laden and I will give you rest". Those who come to him early or late are welcome and equally dear. In the book of Revelation we read that there are city gates to the east and west, north and south. All are bidden to come into God's kingdom. The Rabbis said some enter into the Kingdom of God in one hour, but others hardly in a lifetime. Now let us ask ourselves, how do we react to latecomers? Do we resent them, welcome them, accept or reject them?

Secondly, we consider the compassion of God, that element of tenderness that knows our need of work, of sustenance, of dignity. Our need is not for one twelfth of a day's wages with a worried wife and hungry children to care for, but for our daily bread which God supplies and which we must share. Have we the compassion and generosity that we see in this parable?

Thirdly, we return to the point of fairness. The parable is manifestly not "fair"; it is an illustration of God's bounty and generosity. All receive the same reward for their service, for all service counts the same with God. It is not a matter of the quantity of the service, but the love behind the service is what counts - the love given and received. A child's present of five pence to God is as valuable to Him as our one hundred pounds and possibly touches the heart more. All God gives to us is of grace out of the goodness of his heart. We do not deserve it or earn it. We receive not pay but a gift from God, not a reward but grace.

Shall we begrudge God's generosity, his prodigality? Yes, we still say, "It's not fair" - and we are right, but love, compassion and generosity transcend fairness.

The Cross wasn't fair either, but love conquered!

A25 FORGIVENESS

St. Matthew 6.vv.5-15

~ Whenever you pray, do not be like the hypocrites, for they love to stand and pray in the synagogues, and at the street corners, so that they may be seen by others. Truly I tell you, they have received their reward. But whenever you pray, go into your room and shut the door and pray to your Father who is in

secret, and your Father who sees in secret will reward you. When you are praying, do not heap up empty phrases as the Gentiles do; for they think that they will be heard because of their many words. Do not be like them for your Father knows what you need before you ask him. Pray then in this way: Our Father in heaven, hallowed be your name. Your kingdom come. Your will be done, on earth as it is in heaven. Give us this day our daily bread. And forgive us our debts, as we also have forgiven our debtors. And do not bring us to the time of trial, but rescue us from the evil one.

For if you forgive others their trespasses, your heavenly Father will also forgive you; but if you do not forgive others, neither will your Father forgive your trespasses. ~

It is rather sad if one is remembered only for a saying that seems at first to be wise, but on closer examination is seen to be at the best only a half truth or at the worst a doubtful proposition. Henry Ward Beecher (died 1887) was one of the foremost American preachers and lecturers of his day, and is often remembered for the saying "I can forgive but I cannot forget" is only another way of saying "I cannot forgive". Of course, it depends on how you say it, for if the failure to forget is simply hypocritical and a nursing of one's wrath to keep it warm, as Burns would say, then Henry is quite right.

On the other hand, since active, conscious forgetting is psychologically almost impossible, provided that forgiveness given and received is genuine, it would seem more conducive to spiritual health, progress and peace to treat such memories as infinitely precious memories.

I treasure the memories of forgiveness given and received at human level in so many instances in my life, especially in the contact with family and marriage (where we usually wreak the most havoc!), experiences painful at the time, but not ones that I would like to forget; for our spiritual life is built up not on a vacuum or forgetfulness but on positive memories that warm and encourage us. Such precious memories can and should be a spur to our further spiritual development and interpersonal relationships.

How much more therefore should we treasure the memories of God's forgiveness. It is significant that when Jesus taught His disciples the "Our Father" the only clause which He expanded and elaborated was the need to forgive others as we hope to receive the divine forgiveness. The parable of the Unmerciful Servant in *Matthew 18 vv.21 to end* reinforces this teaching. The account of Corrie Ten Boom forgiving the ex Ravensbruck guard (first she had to pray earnestly for God's forgiveness for herself), and similar modern instances of forgiving love, emphasise the point that when God bids us forgive others He supplies the love which makes it possible for us.

101

Without love there can be no forgiveness, for forgiveness springs from love.

For the Christian, despite the knowledge and conviction that our sins can be and are forgiven, there remains very often a well nigh intractable problem of accepting oneself and becoming a well integrated person, because one is a "haunted person".

There is a tendency for the "unacceptable self" of the past (whose sins, albeit, have been forgiven) to return as a spectre, to trouble the peace of mind of the victim. To treat this "revenant" in a negative way, wishing it to go away, seeking to exorcise it or disregard it, can lead to a morbidity of spirit and psychological dis-ease, for the more one attempts to banish it the stronger becomes the haunting.

By bitter experience, and by the grace of God, I have been led to believe that the solution to this problem lies in accepting the "unacceptable" self in a positive way, (indeed of welcoming the ghost), and seeing in it a signal proof of God's good grace in providing us with an "angel of light", i.e. a token and promise of what by His grace we may become - the spectre is but the foil of that better self which we long to be and by God's grace can become.

A26 BREAD

St. John 6.vv.1-14

~ After this Jesus went to the other side of the Sea of Galilee, also called the Sea of Tiberias. A large crowd kept following him, because they saw the signs that he was doing for the sick. Jesus went up the mountain and sat there with his disciples. Now the Passover, the festival of the Jews, was near. When he looked up and saw a large crowd coming toward him, Jesus said to Philip, "Where are we to buy bread for these people to eat?". He said this to test him, for he himself knew what he was going to do. Philip answered him, "Six months' wages would not buy enough bread for each of them to get a little". One of his disciples, Andrew, Simon Peter's brother, said to him, "There is a lad here who has five barley loaves and two fish. But what are they among so many people?". Jesus said, "Make the people sit down". Now there was a great deal of grass in the place; so they sat down, about five thousand in all. Then Jesus took the loaves, and when he had given thanks, he distributed them to those who were seated; so also the fish, as much as they wanted. When they were satisfied, he told his disciples, "Gather up the fragments left over, so that nothing may be lost". So they gathered them up and from the fragments of the five barley loaves, left by those who had eaten, they filled twelve baskets. When the people saw the sign that he had done, they began to say, "This is indeed the prophet who is come into the world." ~

Victor Hugo recounts the story of a woman and her two children who during the French Revolution were forced to flee their home and take refuge in the forest, subsisting on roots and plants, and hiding away from the soldiery who searched the woods for such refugees. An officer, detecting a movement in the bushes, ordered his sergeant to drag out whoever was hiding. The latter brought the wretched trio before the officer who in pity seeing their hunger and plight offered the woman a roll of bread. Eagerly she seized it and breaking it in half gave it to the children. The sergeant amazed said, "Is it because the mother is not hungry?". "No sergeant", the officer replied, "it is because she is a mother".

We all know the importance of the "Staff of Life" and our dependence upon God the giver of physical and spiritual sustenance and we are all like beggars stretching out our hands to receive bread.

Christ in the first temptation which he tells us about (for the account must originally have come from that lonely figure in the wilderness) rejected the temptation either to satisfy his own physical hunger or to become an "economic Messiah" in order to bring in the Kingdom of God - yet in compassion he fed four and five thousand in the wilderness.

God fed his people with "manna" in the wilderness in the Exodus wanderings. He knows our needs and that we also tend to wander in the wilderness of this life, sad, lost, lonely and dispirited, but he ministers to our needs.

Pope Leo once said, "We become what we eat". The bread of which we are speaking, material or spiritual, comes from outside but we need to take it into ourselves, to digest it, and this applies particularly to the Word of God. We need to digest and be nourished by the Word of God, Jesus himself, who is described in the Gospels as the "Word made Flesh", the "Bread that comes down from Heaven".

In Holy Communion we perceive the greatest of all miracles. We sing "Bread of Heaven on thee we feed". If we take into ourselves the "true bread that comes down from heaven", we receive the gift of eternal life. Little Joe knew this. He was a small boy living in an orphanage. Every month the doctor examined the children to monitor their progress. One day the Sister in Charge said to little Joe, "It's your turn to go in now". When he came out she said to him, "Well, little Joe, and what did the doctor say about you?". "What a miserable little specimen!" was the reply, "but I don't think he knew that I have just taken my first Communion, do you Sister?".

Some people think that a consecrated wafer or piece of bread is the end product of a Communion Service. The end product is rather lives refashioned, reformed, consecrated and transformed.

A27 LOVE

St. John 15.vv.12-17

~ *"This is my commandment, that you love one another as I have loved you. No one has greater love than this, to lay down one's life for one's friends. You are my friends if you do what I command you. I do not call you servants any longer, because the servant does not know what the master is doing; but I have called you friends because I have made known to you everything that I have heard from my Father. You did not choose me but I chose you. And I appointed you to go and bear fruit, fruit that will last, so that the Father will give you whatever you ask in my name. I am giving you these commands so that you may love one another."* ~

The secular world around us recognises perhaps more than ever today the need to love and to be loved. Denied an opportunity to love others, many people today find their lives distorted or unfulfilled. I read recently of a bridge between Cannes and Nice where a bunch of flowers had been placed on the parapet of the bridge in a touching memorial to a rich young girl who drove up in her car, got out of the car clutching her dog, and leapt over the bridge to her death leaving behind a note "Nobody loves me except my dog". We must be assured we matter, or there is no value or purpose to life. The need for love begins at conception and persists through life. A certain doctor in a maternity hospital pinned a note on the cot of an ailing little baby, "This baby is to be loved every three hours". What an insight! A Jew once consulted a Rabbi - "Rabbi, what should I do? My son has given up belief in God". The wise Rabbi replied, "Love him more than ever".

We all acknowledge the need to love and be loved, and we are grieved when we hear of those (usually, but not always) suffering neglect through divorce and broken homes; we feel profoundly sorry for the bereaved, neglected, rejected, lonely and unloved, those who are insecure, who lack a sense of "identity", purpose and peace.

What does the Christian have to say to such? First of all, we must say and prove to them "I love you". You are a brother or sister in Christ. We must show that we care. Actions speak louder than words, but we must go on to prove to them that our love is genuine and based upon something or someone much greater than ourselves.

We must assure them that God is love, that love is at the heart of the universe, that love is immortal and eternal. By our optimism we must demonstrate that we know God is in control of the world, that he cares, and cares infinitely, for us his children, that he is a God of compassion entering into and sharing our grief's and sorrows. Karl Barth, probably one of the greatest theologians of our time, was asked at a conference, "What is the greatest theological truth that you know?". The questioner awaited a profound theological exposition from the great man, but received, after a few moments' thought, the reply, "Jesus loves me".

St. Augustine described love in these terms, "It has hands to help others, feet to hasten to the poor and needy, eyes to see misery and want and ears to hear the sighs and sorrows of mankind." What St. Augustine was describing was his perception of Jesus Christ.

The love of Christ was universal, unconditional, understanding and forgiving. It was a love sacrificial to the utmost and vulnerable as all true love must be to rejection, pain and sorrow yet withal filled with an unconquerable good will and joy that no one can take away.

A28 COURAGE

St. Matthew 10.vv.16-22

~ *Jesus said, "See I am sending you out like sheep into the midst of wolves, so be wise as serpents and innocent as doves. Beware of them, for they will hand you over to councils and flog you in synagogues; and you will be dragged before governors and kings because of me, as a testimony to them and the Gentiles. When they hand you over, do not worry about how you are to speak or what you are to say; for what you are to say will be given to you at the time; for it is not you who speak but the Spirit of the Father speaking through you. Brother will betray brother to death, and a father his children, and children will rise against parents and have them put to death; and you will be hated by all because of my name. But the one who endures to the end will be saved." ~*

The words of Jesus, "Behold I am sending you out as sheep among wolves" do not sound very kind, until we remember that his "service is perfect freedom"; we can refuse to love and serve him; he does not compel us, but those to whom these words were addressed had already cast in their lot with him and were pledged to his service.

Jesus knew moreover that there is something in the Spirit of men and women that rises to meet a challenge. The call of the heroic speaks to our hearts. Sir

105

Ernest Shackleton, setting off for the south pole, was inundated with letters from young and old, rich and poor, of high and low estate, volunteering to share in his venture. They already knew the risks; they had been forewarned. Sir Winston Churchill during the Second World War promised us blood, toil, sweat and tears. His expectations were fully confirmed, but his people survived the ordeal.

Jesus was an absolute realist. He knew the forces of evil ranged against the good. He knew what his followers could expect, nor was he mistaken.

Among some of the earliest martyrs for the Christian faith was the aged Polycarp who, on his way to martyrdom, was urged by friends and enemies to recant, to forswear his faith in Jesus and thus escape with his life. "Eighty and six years have I served him and he has never done me wrong, how then can I deny my Saviour?" said Polycarp and proceeded on his journey to martyrdom.

In the sad history of the Church down through the ages, we read in such a horrifying book as "Fox's Book of Martyrs" the appalling cruelty and suffering to which Christians have been subjected and their courage, and constancy in the faith.

As Jesus predicted, even families have been divided over loyalty to Jesus.

Truly we are not today likely to be called upon to suffer for our faith, but we still need courage to live for Christ. There are many insidious dangers. Society and the unregenerate world are "crooked".

We need courage to stand out, often alone, against the pressures of the world.

How often we hear as an excuse for amoral or immoral behaviour, "Everyone does it", and we need to reply, "No, not everyone. Christians do not, nor shall I". Around us we perceive petty as well as flagrant dishonesty which we must reject. Not only in the media but in other ways too we are reminded that purity in thought, speech and action have all too often given way to coarse and uncouth behaviour with which Christians can have nothing to do.

In all such instances it is necessary to be courageous in rejecting and disapproving of such behaviour, in "standing up and being counted", as we say.

Jesus knew our inner nature and our weaknesses, but he promises us his presence and power, his strength and courage. Only in the assurance of his presence with us can we have the courage to witness faithfully to him and

106

only he could possibly say such a thing as, "I am sending you out like sheep among wolves".

Courage is not a fearlessness born of unthinking instinctive behaviour but of acknowledging the inward fear, facing up to it and believing in him who is so much greater than we are and who has promised us his presence, bringing victory out of our fears.

Victory lies in the knowledge of the presence of God and his Christ.

A29 <u>EVANGELISM</u>

St. Luke 10.vv.1-12

~ After this the Lord appointed seventy others and sent them on ahead of him in pairs to every town and place where he himself intended to go. He said to them, "The harvest is plentiful, but the labourers are few; therefore ask the Lord of the harvest to send out labourers into his harvest. Go on your way. See, I am sending you out like lambs into the midst of wolves. Carry no purse, no bag, no sandals; and greet no one on the road. Whatever house you enter, first say, 'Peace to this house'. And if anyone is there who shares in peace, your peace will rest on that person; but if not, it will return to you. Remain in the same house, eating and drinking whatever they provide, for the labourer deserves to be paid. Do not move about from house to house. Whenever you enter a town and its people welcome you, eat what is set before you; cure the sick who are there, and say to them, "The kingdom of God has come near to you". But whenever you enter a town and they do not welcome you, go out into its streets and say, 'Even the dust of your town that clings to our feet, we wipe off in protest against you. Yet know this; the kingdom of God has come near'. I tell you, on that day it will be more tolerable for Sodom than for that town." ~

In these days when so many people watch football and rugby on the terraces or on the television there is a great awareness of the rules of the game, but someone has coined the phrase "moving the goalposts". Such an idea suggests anarchy; there must be rules, and they must be obeyed.

In the lovely little book of Ruth in the Old Testament do we see a bending of the rules or has someone "moved the goalposts"? Living among the Jewish people, Ruth, a Moabitess, a foreigner, "unclean" and outside the Law, is portrayed as displaying love and loyalty to her Jewish family and neighbours and is accepted; not despised or rejected. Could this mean the "rules of the game" are wrong? Surely God could not accept Gentiles on the same basis as Jews? "Yes", said a few, "that must be it". Has someone moved the goalposts?

Did she not become the great grandmother of the great King David? "Yes", said the many, "Ruth was the 'exception who proved the rule'". Can we draw general conclusions from this particular instance. The rules of the game still stand, but look at it whichever way you choose, there is a problem here.

So the rules did stand until Jesus came on the scene. At first a popular figure, teaching and healing, he soon began to break the rules (or did he move the goalposts?). He mixed with Gentiles and outcasts, praised highly a Roman Centurion, behaved like a Samaritan his enemies said, commended a publican in prayer as against a Pharisee, sent out 70 or 72 apostles into a largely Gentile world teaching a universalism that many of his fellows deplored. "This simply won't do", said the religious authorities, "That's breaking the rules of the game" and so by twisting their own rules they put him to death.

After Pentecost Jesus' followers went out to import the "good news", but how should they "play" it? Some (the majority?) said, "We must obey the Law of Moses. All must accept the Jewish rules, then salvation can be offered". "No", said others, "Jesus came to do away with all old rules; only love counts." There was a sharp division of liberals and hard-liners. Paul, a protagonist of the liberal faction declared, "All that's needed is faith in God and Jesus Christ." Peter, not so sure, could see the value of the old traditions and the reasons for the "rules of the game". But while the Church discussed and argued, God acted. Peter, confronted by the simple fact of Cornelius' faith and his acceptance by the Holy Spirit was forced to drop his prejudice - "Do not call unclean what God counts clean" - that ended the matter.

The Church of Christ is not a "closed shop". However much we believe in the rules of the game, only one rule really counts - the law of love. The Church, past and present, acts sometimes like an exclusive club. But Christ will have none of this exclusive behaviour. The Church must be a community of the redeemed and reconciled, reconciled to God, to one another, and to itself.

We must accept with thanksgiving the diversity of God's world and accept all God's children with love and fellowship - then the rules won't matter for it will be a different game - but the goalposts will be steady!

A30 RICHES

St. Matthew 19.vv.16-26

~ Someone came to Jesus and said, "Teacher, what good deed must I do to have eternal life?". And he said to him, "Why do you ask me about what is good? There is only one who is good. If you wish to enter into life, keep the commandments". He said to him, "Which ones?". And Jesus said, "You shall

not murder; You shall not commit adultery; You shall not steal; You shall not bear false witness; Honour your father and mother; also, You shall love your neighbour as yourself." The young man said to him, "I have kept all these; what do I still lack?". Jesus said to him, "If you wish to be perfect, go and sell your possessions, and give the money to the poor and you will have treasure in heaven; then come follow me." When the young man heard this word, he went away grieving, for he had many possessions. Then Jesus said to his disciples, "Truly, I tell you, it will be hard for a rich man to enter the kingdom of heaven. Again I tell you, it is easier for a camel to go through the eye of a needle than for someone who is rich to enter the kingdom of God." When the disciples heard this they were greatly astounded and said, "Then who can be saved?". But Jesus looked at them and said, "For mortals it is impossible, but for God all things are possible." ~

Some characters flit in and out of the pages of scripture and we hear no more of them. How we would love to know what happened to them later. Here we have the brief but tragic story of a rich young ruler who came to Jesus full of good intentions but went away heavy of heart after Jesus' challenge - and so did Jesus! He was a man, like so many modern men, "possessed by his possessions"!. The love of riches held him back from freedom and true life in the spirit, for he was concerned with doing and not with being.

He had nevertheless observed the commandments of the Old Testament and Jesus appears to have accepted this. Jesus never questioned the validity of the Ten Commandments but he knew that they did not go far enough. The commands are of universal application. They are literally the "Maker's Instructions". They are not suggestions, but categorical imperatives. We flout them at our peril.

In what ways were the Commandments defective? Jesus upheld them but he went far beyond their moral and spiritual dictates for some are negative. "Go and see what Andrew is doing and tell him to stop it", is a sign of our doubts and fears! "Don't touch that tree" is almost an invitation to do the forbidden thing (like touching an electric fence). Nevertheless the Commandments with all their negative injunctions were valued by Our Lord.

The problem concerning the rich young ruler was that he was obsessed with his riches and could not let go. It matters greatly how we obtain our riches and even more what use we make of them. One of the most pernicious doctrines is that the "end justifies the means", and that cannot be sustained. Money is not the root of all evil. Wise stewardship of money and other resources is important in our churches and our personal accounting.

Somehow the idea has arisen that "money is the root of all evil". Not so! No one, least of all St. Paul, said that. The <u>love</u> of money is the root of all evil. It has been rightly pointed out that we cannot take it with us when we go. Jesus' parable about the rich man who pulled down his barns to build greater ones - and almost immediately died is a salutary reminder that we should not amass treasures upon earth. I read recently of two old men discussing the death of a mutual friend. Man "A" said, "I hear old Bert has died; he was rich; do you know how much he left?". The answer of Man "B" was, "He left the lot!".

Not all can manage the wealth that they acquire in wise and generous ways. The advent of the National Lottery has shown how much havoc the acquisition of wealth may cause in peoples' lives. Not only the lives and well-being of others depend upon our wise stewardship of the wealth and resources God provides, but also the matter of what sort of people we ourselves become and our eternal destiny.

A31 ADULTERY

St. John 8.vv.1-11

~ *Early in the morning Jesus came again to the temple. All the people came to him and he sat down and began to teach them. The Scribes and Pharisees brought a woman who had been caught in adultery; and making her stand before all of them, they said to him, "Teacher, this woman was caught in the very act of committing adultery. Now in the law Moses commanded us to stone such women. Now, what do you say?". They said this to test him, so that they might have some charge to bring against him. Jesus bent down and wrote with his finger on the ground. When they kept on questioning him, he straightened up and said to them, "Let anyone among you who is without sin be the first to throw a stone at her". And once again he bent down and wrote on the ground. When they heard it, they went away, one by one, beginning with the elders; and Jesus was left alone with the woman standing before him. Jesus straightened up and said to her, "Woman, where are they? Has no one condemned you?". She said, "No one, sir". and Jesus said, "Neither do I condemn you. Go your way, and from now on do not sin again." ~*

Most Bible scholars are of the opinion that this passage is not part of the original Gospel of St. John, especially since in some ancient manuscripts it is included in St. Luke's Gospel. It has, however, close affinity with the kind of material St. John records of Jesus, and, whatever its source, we are grateful that the episode was recorded and not lost.

The main message of the story is very lovely; though there are some unlovely aspects to the passage. The latter consist in the attitude of the Pharisees and

Scribes towards Jesus and the sinful woman. Jesus is addressed as "Teacher", which coming from them was probably hypocritical, but there is no doubt that they deliberately tried to entrap Jesus when they presented the dilemma, "Do you or do you not subscribe to the Law of Moses?". The implications of condemning or exonerating the woman were fraught with dire consequences, but the insight and skill of Jesus frustrated their evil designs. As for their attitude to the woman, they appear as harsh and censorious; in their minds they had already condemned her to death for her sin. It is true that idolatry, murder and adultery were punished by death in ancient Israel. Indeed in the Book of Numbers we have an account of a man who gathered sticks on the Sabbath and was put to death for his sin! It is, however, unlikely that in Jesus' day the bystanders would have practised lynch law out of fear of their Roman overlords. It appears that these cruel bystanders were playing a devious and very unpleasant "game".

The true greatness and glory of the story lies in the attitude of Jesus towards the bystanders and the woman. Having skilfully avoided the dilemma, Jesus brought home to the accusers their own sinfulness, their secret faults and sense of guilt, so that they all slipped quietly away. As for the woman, we see as always the understanding and compassion that Jesus showed to sinful humanity. Some people mistakenly think that Jesus tacitly condoned the woman's sin. Nothing could be further from the truth. Jesus condemned sin but loved sinners despite their sins. He hated sin but loved sinners. Jesus must have known how much the woman had already been punished in her own conscience and public conviction of guilt. If only we knew the subsequent history of the woman, but that is not to be!

Jesus gave her new life, raised from the "death" of her sin. He gave her new hope. The Gospel of Jesus is the gospel of further chances to become what God willed her to be; for he saw her not simply as a bedraggled and wretched creature condemned to death for her sin, but as one capable of becoming a dear child of God.

A32 SEEING JESUS

St. John 12.vv.20-32

~ Now among those who went up to worship at the festival were some Greeks. They came to Philip from Bethsaida in Galilee, and said to him, "Sir, we wish to see Jesus". Philip went and told Andrew; then Andrew and Philip went and told Jesus. Jesus answered them, "The hour has come for the Son of Man to be glorified. Very truly, I tell you, unless a grain of wheat falls into the ground and dies, it remains a single grain, but if it dies, it bears much fruit. Those who love their life lose it, and those who hate their life in this world

will keep it for eternal life. Whoever serves me must follow me, and where I am, there will my servant be also. Whoever serves me, the Father will honour. Now my soul is troubled. And what should I say - 'Father, save me from this hour?'. No, it is for this reason that I have come to this hour. Father, glorify your name". Then a voice came from heaven, "I have glorified it and I will glorify it again". The crowd standing there heard it and said that it was thunder. Others said, "An angel has spoken to him". Jesus answered, "This voice has come for your sake, not for mine. Now is the judgement of this world; now the ruler of this world will be driven out. And I, when I am lifted up from the earth, will draw all people to myself". ~

"Sir, we would like to see Jesus" - wouldn't we all?

This was fairly easy, for Philip and Andrew could presumably go round the corner and tell Jesus who no doubt was perfectly willing to talk to Greeks or to anyone. What happened, we wonder, to those Greeks? Like so many characters who flit in and out of the Gospel pages, they naturally fade quickly into obscurity because the interest for the Gospel writers is centred upon the figure of Jesus.

We could take this out of context in the twentieth century - imagine a tug at the sleeve and, "Excuse me, I'd like to see Jesus". What are we to do or say, for since the Ascension there is a big difficulty here! Jesus' contemporaries had some advantages with Jesus nearby in person, but they did not know as much about Jesus as we do from records in the new Testament, from theology, from Christian experience of 2,000 years. They may not have known all this, but they must have seen something very extraordinary in this man - it showed.

For <u>his</u> contemporaries it showed in his behaviour - a caring, brave character of utter integrity; in his powers of leadership, drawing others to himself and retaining their loyalty. It showed in his speech. "Never man spake like this man", said his friends and enemies. It showed in his knowledge and insights, "Where does he get all these things (knowledge)?". His mighty works of healing impressed those who witnessed them, "We never saw anything like this before!". The compassion of Jesus, his common touch, his championship of the outcast, the lonely, those who were despised and rejected marked him out as someone very special. Many tributes were paid to him from unexpected sources. The rich young ruler addressed him as "Good Master", several Pharisees accorded him the title "Rabbi" and a Roman Centurion at the Cross described him as "God's Son".

For <u>our</u> contemporaries (again a tug at the sleeve, "I would like to see him <u>now</u>!"), what are we going to do or say about Jesus? Truly we could produce the Gospels but they are not a biography, only fleeting glimpses. We could show pictures of stained glass representations, but how inadequate these would be to portray him. We could point to the saints whose lives Jesus transformed or to modern men and women whose lives reflect a Christ-likeness.

But the awful and terrifying truth is this, that if they want to see the reflection of Christ, they look at us! What a frightful responsibility we bear. It is from us who dare to call ourselves Christians that the world learns about Jesus. Have we really been "changed into his likeness from glory to glory?". Can we say, "I live, yet not I, but Christ lives in me?". Do we show the compassion, sincerity and love of Christ - in short, are we letting the world see him albeit in a somewhat distorting mirror, for that is how Jesus is or is not shown to the world.

A33 SIN

St. Matthew 12.vv.22-32

~ *They brought Jesus a demoniac who was blind and mute; and he cured him, so that the one who had been blind and mute could speak and see. All the crowds were amazed and said, "Can this be the Son of David?". But when the Pharisees heard it, they said, "It is only by Beelzebub, the ruler of demons, that this fellow casts out the demons". He knew what they were thinking and said to them, "Every kingdom divided against itself is laid waste, and no city or house divided against itself will stand. If Satan casts out Satan, he is divided against himself; how then will his kingdom stand? It I cast out demons by Beelzebub, by whom do your own exorcists cast them out? therefore they will be your judges. But if it is by the Spirit of God that I cast out demons, then the kingdom of God has come to you. Or how can one enter a strong man's house and plunder his property, without first tying up the strong man? Then indeed the house can be plundered. Whoever is not with me is against me, and whoever does not gather with me scatters. Therefore I tell you, people will be forgiven for every sin and blasphemy, but blasphemy against the Spirit will not be forgiven. Whoever speaks a word against the Son of Man will be forgiven, but whoever speaks against the Holy Spirit will not be forgiven, either in this age or in the age to come".* ~

At the close of this passage there is a statement by Jesus which has caused a great deal of heart-searching and, indeed, anxiety to those who do not fully understand it. I refer to the "Unforgivable Sin". As Christians we naturally assume (and rightly so) that there is no sin so grievous that God will not forgive it - but we must always remember that God is the one who forgives the sins of "all them that are penitent" and herein is the problem and the

113

answer. Can God possibly or reasonably forgive the sins of those who are not conscious of sin, who do not show remorse for wrong doing, who do not sue for mercy, pardon and peace? It has been said that those who believe they have committed the "unforgivable sin" should be assured that they have not committed it. This may be an over-simplification of the case; but it is true nevertheless.

As a layman, before entering the Ordained Ministry, I used to visit the local prison regularly at least once a week in the evening after work. I was privileged to receive a cell key and to visit freely the prisoners under the Rule 43 category, that is, those who for murder, child abuse or other serious crimes, were shut up for most of the day in their cells for their own protection from other prisoners who might assault them. As a layman, and not a priest, I found that prisoners spoke very readily of their problems. I never probed into their affairs, but often they spoke of their fears that they could never be forgiven their sins (and crimes). To me this was a source of considerable concern, for it was clear that (and I blame them not) they had totally misunderstood the teaching of Jesus about forgiveness. This was a "heaven-sent" opportunity to stress that only if their hearts were hardened so that they felt no remorse or sense of guilt, and only if they persisted in self-justification and resisted the invitation of Christ to confess their sins and receive pardon and peace - only so could they possibly be said to have committed a sin which cannot be forgiven. God does not compel us to confess our sins, nor can he forgive sins that we do not acknowledge.

It is unfortunate (to say the least) that the word "repent" is so often used in a negative sense, that is, in repining, making oneself miserable with the memory of past wrongdoing, instead of grasping the opportunity of renewal offered to us in God's forgiveness of our sins. Repentance or "metanoia" involves a positive dynamic, a radical renewal of heart, mind, soul, of way of life, of relationship with God, others and ourselves.

Not only does forgiveness accepted bring pardon and peace to those who receive it from Christ, but casebooks of doctors, psychologists and psychiatrists recount numerous cases of those who, receiving forgiveness from God and their fellows, have gained physical healing when their feelings of anxiety and guilt have been allayed and they have gained that sense of pardon and peace that God wills for all his children - the peace that passes all understanding.

The "unforgivable sin" is a persistent and hardened rejection of the proffered love of God and his forgiveness, a wilful refusal to acknowledge guilt and to accept the gift of pardon which God in his grace offers to us.

A34 PRIDE

St. Luke 18.vv.9-14

~ *Jesus also told this parable to some who trusted in themselves that they were righteous and regarded others with contempt. "Two men went up to the temple to pray, one a Pharisee and the other a tax collector. The Pharisee, standing by himself, was praying thus, 'God I thank you that I am not like other people; thieves, rogues, adulterers, or even like this tax collector. I fast twice a week; I give a tenth of all my income'. But the tax collector, standing far off, would not even look up to heaven, but was beating his breast and saying, 'God, be merciful to me, a sinner!'. I tell you, this man went down to his home justified rather than the other; for all who exalt themselves will be humbled, but all who humble themselves will be exalted".* ~

All would agree that Jesus was a master storyteller. His stories were so vivid and lifelike that quite often it is difficult to distinguish between story and event. Among the purposes of Jesus' stories is the eradication of wrong ideas and the implanting of new.

The story of the Pharisee and Publican praying in the Temple is a wonderful example of teaching about the efficacy of prayer.

So great was the veneration of the Temple that the Pharisee would go up at 9am, 12 noon and 3pm to pray there. The Pharisee, we are told, prayed "with himself" giving a testimonial before God of his merits, a kind of monologue. He describes how he went beyond the strict requirements of the Law. There was only one obligatory fast on Yom Kippur but he fasted on Monday and Thursday - market day (when Jerusalem was full and a good audience might see the whitened faces and dishevelled clothes of those who fasted). He also tithed beyond the Law's demand. His whole attitude was typical of the worst in Pharisaism. A certain Rabbi Simeon ben Jocai once said, "If there are only two righteous men in the world, I and my son are they; but if only one, I am he!". The attitude of the Pharisee was completely wrong for he showed no sense of need; he was self-sufficient and felt no need of God or God's mercy and forgiveness. He went to inform God how good he was.

The publican (tax collector) on the other hand, one of the despised in Jewry, was aware of his sin. He knew he was an outcast and would not even lift his eyes to heaven but cried, "O God, be merciful to me a sinner". He asks for nothing but mercy, the only thing he dared to ask for. The cry of deep need reaches God's ears. He is welcomed into God's family and new life.

115

No one who is proud can truly pray. The gate of heaven is so low that we can enter only on our knees. At the Church of the Nativity in Bethlehem one cannot enter in unless one stoops. A sculptor when depicting Jesus on the cross carved the face with the head bowed so low upon the chest that only by kneeling down and looking up can one look upon the face of the crucified.

No one who despises his fellows truly prays. We are one with the whole of sinful, suffering, sorrowing humanity.

True prayer arises from setting our lives beside the life of Christ. All the Pharisee said was probably true - a paragon of respectability, but the question should not be "how do I compare with other people?", but "how do I compare with Jesus?".

If we set our lives beside his, all we can say is, "Lord, have mercy". To confess our sins is not to tell God something he doesn't know, but humbly to acknowledge our sins before God brings pardon and peace.

A35 PARALYTIC

St. Mark 2.vv.1-12

~ *When Jesus returned to Capernaum after some days, it was reported that he was at home. So many gathered around that there was no longer room for them, not even in front of the door; and he was speaking the word to them. Then some people came, bringing to him a paralysed man, carried by four of them. And when they could not bring him to Jesus because of the crowd, they removed the roof above him; and after having dug through it, they let down the mat on which the paralytic lay. When Jesus saw their faith, he said to the paralytic, "Son, your sins are forgiven". Now some of the Scribes were sitting there, questioning in their hearts, "Why does this fellow speak in this way? It is blasphemy! Who can forgive sins but God alone?". At once Jesus perceived in his spirit that they were discussing these questions among themselves; and he said to them, "Why do you raise such questions in your hearts? Which is easier, to say to the paralytic, 'Your sins are forgiven', or to say, 'Stand up and take your mat and walk'? But so that you may know that the Son of Man has authority on earth to forgive sins", he said to the paralytic, "I say to you, stand up, take your mat and go to your home". And he stood up and immediately took the mat and went out before all of them: so that they were all amazed and glorified God, saying, "We have never seen anything like this!".* ~

This lovely story of one of Jesus' healing miracles is full of tenderness and spiritual insights. "My son, your sins are forgiven", is like a response to an unspoken appeal, for the paralytic had not asked for healing but Jesus knew his need and the reason why he was confined to his bed.

At no point in the story do we have even a hint of the man's faith, or lack of it. His friends show their faith and determination. The Greek word for "opened up" the roof in this Gospel is dug out. How much structural damage they caused we do not know; it was probably quite considerable, but all worthwhile if their faith in Jesus the healer was to be justified and their friend healed. There is here an important lesson for us; we must in faith bring others to Christ. We cannot heal; only God can, but we can and should co-operate with God by bringing before him in prayer our friends, sick or in need.

It is surprising that even in these (enlightened?) days there is still such confusion in the minds even of Christians about the connection between sin and suffering. The Rabbis of old said there can be no healing until all sins are forgiven. This is at the best only a partial truth, based upon the erroneous presumption that all suffering is due to the sin of the sufferer. We must acknowledge the fact that not all suffering can be so readily explained. Did not Christ die for our sins, that is because of them? The Book of Job, that spiritual masterpiece of the Old Testament, sheds welcome light on the mystery of suffering as Job protested his innocence. On the other hand, we must accept the fact so often recognised by doctors and psychiatrists that a great deal of pain and suffering is attributable to a sense of guilt or sin not forgiven in the mind of the sufferer.

Jesus by his spiritual insight knew that the paralytic needed to know that God was his friend and not his enemy; he needed to find peace and healing, to know that he was not estranged from God. When he heard those gracious and loving words from Jesus, the man felt his burden of sin lifted and, like a child in the dark when someone comes to his aid, received reassurance and comfort, the prerequisite of his healing.

For me the most intriguing part of the story is the situation that arises (or one can imagine it arising) when Jesus in our modern parlance "put his reputation on the line". Sensing the unspoken criticism of some Scribes who were present, Jesus offers to prove his authority to forgive sins by doing what would appear to them to be the more difficult feat - that is, healing the man. I have often speculated upon the atmosphere of doubt, hope, disbelief and incredulity, that must have ensued until Jesus told the man to take up his bed and walk.

On one thing I have no need to speculate, for St. Mark tells us plainly of the amazement of those present, "We have never seen anything like this!".

117

We must bring our sick to Jesus for healing. "Lord to whom else can we go. You have the words of eternal life".

A36 NO SIGN

St. Matthew 12.vv.39-42

~ Then some of the Scribes and Pharisees said to Jesus, "Teacher, we wish to see a sign from you". But he answered them, "An evil and adulterous generation asks for a sign, but no sign will be given to it except the sign of the prophet Jonah. For just as Jonah was three days and three nights in the belly of the sea monster, so for three days and three nights the Son of Man will be in the heart of the earth. The people of Nineveh will rise up at the judgement of Jonah, and see, something greater than Jonah is here! The queen of the South will rise up at the judgement with this generation and condemn it, because she came from the ends of the earth to listen to the wisdom of Solomon, and see, something greater than Solomon is here!" ~

Asking for a "sign" was a tendency of the time of Jesus among people of a religious cast of mind. The Pharisees and Sadducees in particular were anxious to see signs; they desire to see God in the abnormal. Jesus said no sign would be given to overcome their doubts, for they have already received signs but are "blind". For Jesus the signs of God at work can be seen in the flowers, the corn, the yeast, the splendour of common life, the daily miracles around us. The poet has said, "One asked a sign from God, and day by day the sun arose in pearl, in scarlet set; each night the stars appeared in bright array; each morn the thirsty grass with dew was wet; the corn failed not its harvest, nor the vine; and yet he saw no sign". There are none so blind as those who will not see, we say. Poor John Baptist shut up in prison could not see, but Jesus reminded him how "the lame walked, the lepers are cleansed, the deaf hear, the dumb speak ... God is active all around us".

Nevertheless in the Old Testament we have several references to what is called "Deus absconditus", that is, the "hidden God". Job said, "O that I knew where I might find him, that I might even come before his presence". Isaiah said, "Truly thou art a God that hidest thyself". With them we may have sympathy but for their faith we must have admiration.

What a difference it made when Jesus himself came to reveal the Father's love and concern for his children!

"He that hath seen me has seen the Father", Jesus said to Philip. "Come unto me", said Jesus. "Thou hast the words of eternal life. To whom else can we go?", asked Peter. "No man has seen God at any time", says the Fourth Evangelist, "but he who is in the bosom of the Father has made him known".

We may not see Jesus in his earthly ministry, but who can possibly doubt, with such evidence as the Gospels before us, the picture we receive of the one who moved around the streets and villages of Galilee bending over the sick, laying his healing hand upon a leper, comforting the poor and sad, talking to wayfarers and sinners, offering forgiveness, lifting those who lay in the dust and raising them to new hope, teaching, denouncing hypocrisy and sham, battling with evil, hanging upon a cross yet praying for his enemies, conquering pain, hatred and death and returning victorious to his Father's side.

Across that lovely life one word only can be written and that is "Love". "He that hath seen me hath seen the Father". God is love, he cares and his compassion never fails.

Only by faith, that is, putting our hands into God's hands and entrusting our lives to him can we really have the sign or proof of his great love for all his children.

A37 NEW WINE

St. John 2.vv.1-11

~ On the third day there was a wedding in Cana of Galilee, and the mother of Jesus was there. Jesus and his disciples had also been invited to the wedding. When the wine gave out, the mother of Jesus said to him, "They have no wine". And Jesus said to her, "Woman, what concern is that to you and to me? My hour has not yet come". His mother said to the servants, "Do whatever he tells you". Now standing there were six stone water jars for the Jewish rites of purification, each holding twenty or thirty gallons. Jesus said to them, "Fill the jars with water". And they filled them up to the brim. He said to them, "Now draw some out, and take it to the chief steward". So they took it. When the steward tasted the water that had become wine, and did not know where it came from (though the servants who had drawn the water knew), the steward called the bridegroom and said to him, "Everyone serves the good wine first, and then the inferior wine after the guests have become drunk. But you have kept the good wine until now". Jesus did this, the first of his signs, in Cana of Galilee and revealed his glory; and his disciples believed in him. ~

I read recently that a poll among the British people showed that 87% of the population claim to have a higher than average sense of humour! This makes one wonder where the "average" lies! As a schoolboy I was introduced to the idea that the British people according to most Europeans "take their pleasures sadly", and that the further north one goes the less is the joy and sense of fun in life. Certainly some Mediterranean peoples surpass others in this respect. Certainly the Jewish people have always known how to enjoy themselves especially at weddings.

We who are more staid and formal do not share the Jewish wedding festivities; the bright canopy, the lights, the torches, the processions, the feasting often day after day, the open house accorded to the wedding guests by the married couple who are accorded the role of "King and Queen" and exempted from military and other duties for as much as a year. Friends of mine who have attended such festivities have found themselves incapable of keeping up with the prolonged feasting and merriment. There is, however, one essential ingredient in all this - and that is <u>wine</u>. The Rabbis say that without wine there is no joy and joy is the keynote of the changing of water into wine at Cana in Galilee. But let it first be stressed that drunkenness and drinking to excess have never been a part of wedding festivities. Such an abuse of wine would be regarded with severe reproof. Wine was always diluted - two parts water to three parts wine - so those who imagine Jesus approved of excess alcoholic consumption need to think again!

But what was taking place at this wedding.? St. John describes it as a "sign", which means that we must not press too hard the details of the story. Jesus as a guest would naturally have sympathy with the Governor of the feast and the embarrassment of the family and no doubt he would wish to help - but why with 180 gallons of wine (1,000 bottles)? What is St. John trying to tell us in this "sign"?

Surely he is telling us what he has already told us before, namely, that with the coming of Jesus something new, something transcending all the glory and blessings of the past has broken into the world; the old "water" of Judaism has become the new "wine" of Christianity; Jesus Christ is offering to mankind boundless grace; the new order brings blessings enough and to spare for all the needs of mankind; God in Christ is a super-abundant giver of all good gifts, the old order has passed away; new light, new joys are being shed upon mankind. "Behold, I make all things new". When Christ comes life sparkles anew for there is joy and gladness.

In the Victoria and Albert Museum there is a terracotta figure of Jesus and his mother. Mary looks at the child with joy and the child Jesus looks out at us (as in icons) with merriment. The Italian creator of the figure must have known the joy that for the Christian lies at the heart of creation.

A38 BLINDNESS

St. Mark 10.vv.46-52

~ They came to Jericho. As Jesus and his disciples and a large crowd were leaving Jericho, Bartimaeus son of Timaeus, a blind beggar, was sitting by the roadside. When he heard that it was Jesus of Nazareth, be began to shout out and say, "Jesus, Son of David, have mercy on me!". Many sternly ordered him to be quiet, but he cried out even more loudly, "Son of David, have mercy on me!". Jesus stood still and said, "Call him here". And they called the blind man, saying to him, "Take heart; get up, he is calling you". So throwing off his cloak, he sprang up and came to Jesus. Then Jesus said to him, "What do you want me to do for you?". The blind man said to him, "My Teacher, let me see again". Jesus said to him, "Go; your faith has made you well". Immediately he regained his sight and followed him on the way. ~

St. Mark records the lovely story of Blind Bartimaeus. Jesus was nearing Jerusalem and the Cross, yet despite the crowds on the road, it appears that only these two were communicating, so deep was the intimacy. It is a story of patience and compassion. Bartimaeus was not going to miss this heaven-sent opportunity to regain his sight.

In a strange way we become involved in the story for we identify so closely with the beggar. There is a sense in which we are all beggars and blind too. We hear the Lord passing by on his way to the Cross but because of the dullness of our blinded sight we do not understand what it means to him and to the world; our need is so clamant that we cry out "Lord, that I may receive my sight!".

Physical blindness was, and still is, a tragedy and scourge, but worse by far is the appalling lack of spiritual insight of which we are so often guilty.

Spiritual blindness may result from <u>fear</u>, as was the case with Elisha's Servant at Dotham, a case of blind panic or anxiety when our nerve fails and we lose trust in God's love and care.

When Mary Magdala spoke to Jesus at the tomb on Resurrection morning, in her personal grief and sorrow she was blinded by her tears until the word "Mary" restored her sight.

How blind we often are to our own shortcomings and deficiencies. Robert Burns said, "O wad some power the giftie gie us, to see ourselves as others see us". Pride is often our besetting sin, as Jesus reminds us in the teaching

121

about the mote or speck in the eye of others that we with a beam in our own eye seek to remove!

Often Jesus upbraided the Pharisees and Sadducees for their ignorance and wilful blindness. In John Chapter 9.vv.40-41 some Pharisees asked, "Are we also blind?". Jesus replied, "If you were blind, you would have no guilt; but now that you say, 'We see', your guilt remains". On another occasion he described them as "straining out a gnat and swallowing a camel" (humorous "digs" as so often) but, like "not seeing the wood for the trees", describing a common failing.

Two contrasting cases of blindness through obsession are Saul on the Damascus road consumed by his hatred of the followers of "the Way", and terrorists blinded by hate, ignorance, fear or prejudice, who see only the "sacredness" of their own cause but not the cruelty they inflict.

There is also a wilful blindness; "None so blind as those who won't see". We may shut out deliberately the misery and plight of those around us refusing to become involved because "we have troubles enough of our own".

Whatever may be the cause of our blindness, we need to echo the beggar's cry, "Lord, that I may receive my sight".

For Bartimaeus the first face that he saw was the face of Christ; so shall we too see the glory of God in the face of Jesus Christ.

When we can truly see, we shall gain increased awareness and perception in the light of Christ and follow in the way that leads to eternal life.

A39 THE WORLD

St. John 15.vv.18-27

~ Jesus said, "If the world hates you, be aware that it hated me before it hated you. If you belonged to the world, the world would love you as its own. Because you do not belong to the world, but I have chosen you out of the world - therefore the world hates you. Remember the word that I said to you, 'Servants are not greater than their master'. If they persecuted me, they will persecute you; if they kept my word, they will keep yours also. But they will do all these things to you on account of my name, because they do not know him who sent me. If I had not come and spoken to them, they would not have sin; but now they have no excuse for their sin. Whoever hates me hates my Father also. If I had not done among them the works that no one else did, they would

not have sin. But now they have seen and hated both me and my Father. It was to fulfil the word that is written in their law, 'They hated me without a cause'. When the advocate comes, whom I will send to you from the Father, the Spirit of truth who comes from the Father, he will testify on my behalf. You also are to testify because you have been with me from the beginning." ~

"If the world hates you, remember that it hated me before you".

Must there be antipathy between Christ and the world? Is not God's world good?

Perhaps, like all God's gifts, the world is subject to man's abuse and corruption though basically good in its nature. If, as we believe, Christ's words are true, it follows that if we are truly Christians in this "naughty" world, there is an inevitability about our being in conflict with the world. Many times Jesus predicted that his followers would suffer persecution. The reason for this was that his followers were not "of the world". This does not mean that they were to hate or despise the world, for God made it and it is good; but, as so often in the writing of the Fourth Gospel, the word "world" refers to the <u>unregenerate</u> sinful generality of mankind.

In the moral and spiritual teaching of Jesus, especially in the Sermon on the Mount, Jesus reverses many of the accepted standards of the world. His ethical and spiritual teaching turns upside down the accepted values and norms of his day and of every age.

The Church, therefore, if it is loyal to Christ, challenges the assumption, attitudes and motives of worldly people. The Church, if true to itself, is a disturbing influence in the world.

Two examples of this in the Christian tradition, in a supposedly Christian culture, are the Earl of Shaftesbury who called into question the issue of poverty and became a thorn in the flesh of the established Church, and Wilberforce in his opposition to slavery. Elizabeth Fry, Florence Nightingale and many other nineteenth century reformers may be cited. Those who publicly refute vice and campaign against impurity in our own day are often subject to ridicule and hostility. Christians are obviously not the easiest people to get on with among those who belong to the unregenerate world. People are often uncomfortable in the presence of committed Christian people until they have decided whether to love or hate them.

Among the paradoxical and bewildering statements which abound in the Bible may be cited the apparently contradictory statements that, (a) God so loved the world that he gave his only begotten son, to the end that all that believe in him should not perish but have everlasting life", and, (b) "Fight against sin, the world and the devil". The short and simple answer is that, as so often in the New Testament (especially in the Johannine writings), the word "world" connotes the unredeemed world, the world that leaves God out of account, the world that spurns God's love, that resists the prompting of the Holy Spirit.

Christian people promise either personally or by proxy at their Baptism and Confirmation to fight against the (unregenerate) world, the flesh and the devil. Some of the antipathy directed against true Christians may result from envy deep-seated, an envy of their goodness, their sense of identity, purpose, joy, peace and love.

Envy, however, may be a powerful stimulus to conversion, for one of the most potent influences in Christian conversion is the "envy" (not a "deadly sin") non-Christians may feel when they contemplate the peace and joy of true Christian living.

"Ecclesia" our word for "Church" means a "calling out"; Christians are "called out" from the world; but their love for the world must ever remain as that of God who "so loved the world that he did not (as someone has wryly put it) send a committee!".

A40   GOD CALLS

St. John 1.vv.35-51

~ The next day John again was standing with two of his disciples, and as he watched Jesus walk by, he exclaimed, "Look, here is the Lamb of God!". The two disciples heard him say this, and they followed Jesus. When Jesus turned and saw them following, he said to them, "What are you looking for?". They said to him, "Rabbi (which translated means Teacher), where are you staying?". He said to them, "Come and see". They came and saw where he was staying, and they remained with him that day. It was about four o'clock in the afternoon. One of the two who heard John speak and followed him was Andrew, Simon Peter's brother. He first found his brother Simon and said to him, "We have found the Messiah" (which is translated Anointed). He brought Simon to Jesus, who looked at him and said, "You are Simon son of John. You are to be called Cephas" (which is translated Peter).

The next day Jesus decided to go to Galilee. He found Philip and said to him, "Follow me". Now Philip was from Bethsaida, the city of Andrew and Peter. Philip found Nathanael and said to him, "We have found him about whom Moses in the law and also the prophets wrote, Jesus son of Joseph from Nazareth". Nathanael said to him, "Can anything good come out of

Nazareth?". Philip said to him, "Come and see". When Jesus saw Nathanael coming towards him, he said of him, "Here is truly an Israelite in whom there is no deceit!". Nathanael asked him, "Where did you get to know me?". Jesus answered, "I saw you under the fig tree before Philip called you". Nathanael replied, "Rabbi, you are the Son of God! You are the King of Israel!". Jesus answered, "Do you believe because I told you that I saw you under the fig tree? You will see greater things than these. And he said to him, "Very truly, I tell you, you will see heaven opened and the angels of God ascending and descending upon the Son of Man". ~

What a pity it is that a "vocation to the ministry" so often implies a calling to be ordained. All Christians are called to the service of Christ, to personal commitment to him, to witness and to "evangelise", that is, to declare by word and deed his saving love.

However the call may come whether it be by an inner conviction or by a direct invitation from friends and family or fellow Christians, our response is all important.

In the Old Testament we read of Jeremiah shrinking from God's call but God overcomes his reluctance with the unanswerable pledge, "I will be with you. I will teach you what to say". We may struggle but God is stronger. Saul on the Damascus road ceases to struggle against God. His zeal in persecuting Christians is used by God and his conversion to "the Way" was so complete that he obeyed immediately. Peter and the three fishermen readily obeyed the call. Their readiness, as St. John tells us, arose from their introduction to Jesus by John the Baptist. In all our mission work, like John, we point to Jesus and introduce others to Jesus.

Maybe we are not called like Jeremiah in a position of power and authority to denounce sin; nor are we called like Saul (St. Paul) to travel the Middle East refuting heresies and building up the Church of Christ by argument and example; we may not ,like the disciples of Jesus, be sent out as Apostles into the world. It <u>may</u> be like that, but much more likely, we are called to live quietly and to testify by deed and word to God's love for us and all his children, to the sense of purpose that God has for our lives, what he has done for us in Christ and to the sense of his presence in our lives. This is how we draw close to God and draw others to his saving grace in Jesus Christ.

When we contemplate our own incompetence, our lack of faith, our ignorance and sin, we may well wonder what God can possibly see in us that he calls us to his service. It was not only Moses, Jeremiah and many Old Testament prophets who balked at the thought of becoming spokesmen for God. If God calls us (and he does) he knows us through and through. His promise is always "I am with you". He knows what he can and desires to make of us. A master musician can produce the most wonderful music from a very poor instrument. Fritz Kreisler, the great violinist, maintained that it was the player not the instrument that called forth perfect music. Many doubted that he could succeed with an inferior instrument. In New York he advertised a concert played on a "superb instrument". At the end of his recital there was rapturous applause. When it had died down he raised his violin over his head and smashed it over his knees. There was a stunned silence, then Kreisler said, "It's all right, my good violin is in my dressing room; I bought this for three dollars round the corner".

If Kreisler could produce such results from an inferior instrument, just think what God can make of you or me!

A41 THE WAY

St. John 10.vv.1-10

~ Jesus said, "Very truly", I tell you, anyone who does not enter the sheepfold by the gate but climbs in by another way is a thief and a bandit. The one who enters by the gate is the shepherd of the sheep. The gatekeeper opens the gate for him, and the sheep hear his voice. He calls his own sheep by name and leads them out. When he has brought out all his own, he goes ahead of them, and the sheep follow him because they know his voice. They will not follow a stranger, but they will run from him because they do not know the voice of strangers. Jesus used this figure of speech with them, but they did not understand what he was saying to them. So again Jesus said to them, "Very truly, I tell you, I am the gate for the sheep. All who came before me are thieves and bandits; but the sheep did not listen to them. I am the gate. Whoever enters by me will be saved, and will come in and go out and find pasture. The thief comes only to steal and kill and destroy. I came that they may have life, and have it abundantly." ~

Jesus said, "I am the Way, the Truth and the Life" *(John 14.v6)*. What more could we desire? Has not Jesus fulfilled (indeed transcended) all our aspirations, all that we crave in life? What more could he bestow upon us?

In the Old Testament one of the most frequent words is "Way". The ancient Jew, like his descendants and all people everywhere, sought their way in life, their path to peace and to God the perfecter of their peace. No one wishes to be lost on their pilgrimage through life. "Teach me your way, O Lord", says the Psalmist. The leaders and prophets of the Old Testament were convinced that God directed people in the way they should go. "You will hear a voice behind you saying, 'This is the way; walk in it. Turn neither to right or left'".

But God does more than point out the way, for he promises to lead and be with his people on their journey. One can understand Moses saying, "If you will not go with us, we will not go!". How often I have lost my way when driving or walking but have asked the way and been told so cheerfully and generously, "Come with me. I'll take you there", or, "Follow me; it's not far out of my way". Jesus often said, "Follow me", and he still invites us to put our hand in his on what is so often a hazardous and thorny way through life. He is our constant companion, He does not simply point out the way. As our text implies - he personifies the Way - he is the Way.

"Teach me thy way that I may walk in they truth", says the Psalmist. "I have chosen the way of truth". We all hope that we teach the truth to others but none other than Jesus himself could claim to personify truth. Pilate asked, "What is truth?", not realising that the Truth stood before him in the person of Jesus Christ. "The truth will set you free", said Jesus on one occasion. We long for that freedom from ignorance, fear, and suspicion that we may know the truth about our identity, our purpose in life. Jesus tells us the truth about ourselves, about God's purposes for us, his care for us, his nature and his name of love. Jesus reveals the Father, "He that hath seen me hath seen the Father", Jesus told Philip.

"Thou dost show me the path of life", says the Psalmist. What we seek is not "existence", it is ours already; nor do we crave everlasting life. What we seek is what Jesus offers us. "I am come that they may have life and that they may have it more abundantly". This is life eternal - a life full, free, abundant, meaningful, a new dimension to life, spiritual life, life with a capital "Z". "Zoe" (Aionios) the life of aeons, eternal life.

Jesus, then, shows us the way to God and peace.

Jesus shows us God.

Jesus offers us Life Eternal.

What more could we desire?

A42 CALL OF LEVI

St. Mark 2.vv.13-17

~ *Jesus went out again beside the sea; the whole crowd gathered around him, and he taught them. As he was walking along, he saw Levi son of Alphaeus sitting at the tax booth, and he said to him, "Follow me". And he got up and followed him. And as he sat at dinner in Levi's house, many tax collectors and sinners were also sitting with Jesus and his disciples for there were many who followed him. When the Scribes of the Pharisees saw that he was eating with sinners and tax collectors, they said to his disciples, "Why does he eat with tax collectors and sinners?". When Jesus heard this he said to them, "Those who are well have no need of a physician, but those who are sick; I have come to call not the righteous but sinners".* ~

More than 50 years after the end of World War II, Nazi collaborators are still being hounded and brought to trial; the hatred still persists. The ancient Jews hated collaborators with Rome and a tax collector was a prime target for their hate. To be ruled by Rome was one thing (and very grievous to be borne) but to have to pay for it quite another, for taxation was for the benefit of the Roman overlords.

We (or most of us) pay taxes grudgingly, though we receive good services for our tax. We can, therefore, imagine the odium in which Levi and other tax collectors were held. To add to this, the taxation system was basically dishonest. The Roman system of farming out taxes meant that if you bid a high enough figure, no one asked how much extra you extorted to line your own pocket. Levi, therefore, was classed as among those from whom in modern parlance you "wouldn't buy a second-hand car!".

Levi was a "social leper"; there was no place for him among respectable Jews. To be a social outcast is a most appalling experience. Hugh Redwood recounts how a Chinese woman with a half-caste baby joined a Church, but after a while her past caught up with her and she was rejected. "Is there no place where a sinner is welcome?", she cried. Fortunately the Salvation Army came to her aid.

Levi might well have cried similarly but Jesus "took" him, the last person we'd expect. His reaction to Jesus' kindness and concern is most marked - Jesus did not ask for references or testimonials. Jesus knew what he could make of Levi (as of us too). Jesus knew he could make him acceptable to the other eleven disciples. Jesus knew that every "saint has a past and every sinner a future".

Jesus bade him, "Follow me". The Rabbis too were followed by their disciples but not all followers threw up their livelihoods. When Jesus said "Follow me", he knew what he was asking. He knew his man. In the game of "follow my leader" children must follow every action of the leader, even danger. For Jesus and Levi this was important. Jesus warned his disciples that his way was the way of the Cross.

Who was this "Levi"? None other than the Evangelist, St. Matthew. What did St. Matthew (or Levi) renounce? In the first place he gave up a good, steady, secure employment and a well paid post. His reward was to be pain and sorrow with Jesus but also forgiveness, purpose, love and peace with his new Master.

What is our debt to St. Matthew?

First, we commend his example of courage and decision, taken in the face of adversity. Secondly, he "took his pen" with him. St. Mark may have written the first Gospel, but expanded and added to by St. Matthew, this soon became the basis of the Gospel of St. Matthew, accorded first place and honour in the canon of New Testament scripture.

What a debt we owe to Levi who heard and responded to the call of Jesus Christ!

A43 REMEMBRANCE

St. Luke 23.vv.32-43

~ *Two others also, who were criminals, were led away to be put to death with Jesus. When they came to the place that is called The Skull, they crucified Jesus there with the criminals, one on his right and one on his left. Then Jesus said, "Father, forgive them; for they do not know what they are doing". And they cast lots to divide his clothing. And the people stood by, watching; but the leaders scoffed at him, saying, "He saved others; let him save himself if he is the Messiah of God, his chosen one!". The soldiers also mocked him, coming up and offering him sour wine, and saying, "If you are the King of the Jews, save yourself!". There was also an inscription over him, "This is the King of the Jews". One of the criminals who were hanged there kept deriding him and saying, "Are you not the Messiah? Save yourself and us!". But the other rebuked him, saying, "Do you not fear God, since you are under the same condemnation? And we indeed have been condemned justly, for we are getting what we deserve for our deeds, but this man has done nothing wrong". Then he said, "Jesus, remember me when you come into your kingdom". He replied, "Truly I tell you, today you will be with me in Paradise".* ~

"We will remember them". Why? What is the purpose of it all? Memory is a precious gift, a powerful force for good or evil. There are some memories we would prefer to forget but we are continually bidden to remember.

Memory is a strange phenomenon. Especially in old age our memories of olden times remain, but what we did recently recedes into oblivion, so we remember our nursery rhymes and stories and lessons of our youth but forget the names of people we were introduced to yesterday. Sometimes the strength of our memories is dependent upon the traumas of experience. For many of us war experiences of 50 years ago remain as fresh memories.

Some memories we would prefer to forget, especially those associated with shame and failure, those which leave us with a guilty conscience.

Nevertheless we are continually bidden to remember some things, e.g. November 5th, to pay rates, TV licence, observe the Highway Code, the level in the car park where we left the car, Lot's wife, Remember "Dust thou art and to dust shalt thou return". All these mean "Let this be a lesson to you and profit from past mistakes".

Many memories are sorrowful and refuse to fade, so that grief and emptiness remain, e.g.: we still mourn for young lives ended prematurely and with those who mourn them; peoples' lives shattered by the telegram "We regret to inform you .... a husband/son/fiance ... killed in action"; survivors with bodies and minds shattered.

That is one side of the coin; now turn it over and see; time robs us of people, places, personal happiness, but with memory we may have them for ever; we remember with joy and thanksgiving the willing sacrifices people have made for us - the world with all its faults yet relatively at peace; the sacrifice of our Lord, his atoning death; God's love for his world, inspiring love in his children through the compassion of Christ; at the Eucharist "Do this is remembrance".

Life is a kaleidoscope of ever-changing patterns of sorrow and joy, pain and pleasure - yet one thing is constant - the love and goodness of the Lord. For Christians (the only people who have any sure grounds for optimism in the world) memories good and bad are precious, for we believe in the ultimate victory of the loving purposes of God.

A44 SAINT PETER

St. John 21.vv.15-22

~ *When they had finished breakfast, Jesus said to Simon Peter, "Simon son of John, do you love me more than these?". He said to him, "Yes, Lord; you know that I love you". Jesus said to him, "Feed my lambs". A second time he said to him, "Simon son of John, do you love me?" He said to him, "Yes, Lord; you know that I love you". Jesus said to him, "Tend my sheep". He said to him the third time, "Simon son of John, do you love me?". Peter felt hurt because he said to him the third time, "Simon son of John, do you love me?". And he said to him, "Lord, you know everything; you know that I love you". Jesus said to him, "Feed my sheep. Very truly, I tell you, when you were younger, you used to fasten your own belt and to go wherever you wished. But when you grow old, you will stretch out your hands, and someone else will fasten a belt round you, and take you where you do not wish to go". (He said this to indicate the kind of death by which he would glorify God). After this he said to him, "Follow me". Peter turned and saw the disciple whom Jesus loved following them; he was the one who had reclined next to Jesus at the supper and had said, "Lord, who is it that is going to betray you?". When Peter saw him, he said to Jesus, "Lord, what about him?". Jesus said to him, "If it is my will that he remain until I come, what is that to you? Follow me". ~*

I once saw a poster depicting a little girl painting a picture which seemed to be a mass of undifferentiated colour. She had splotches of paint on her face and her pinafore, but the caption below read, "Please be patient. God hasn't finished with me yet".

This is the subject of our Bible passage. Already the Risen Christ had given proof of the Resurrection to Thomas - now he gives Peter the chance to reaffirm his love for his Master. Three times Peter had denied his Master shortly before the Crucifixion. We cannot fully imagine the awful harrowing sense of guilt that must have haunted poor Peter, but we may be certain that Jesus understood, and for those three occasions of denial, Peter is given the chance three times to declare his love, "Simon, son of John, do you love me?".

It has not escaped the notice of New Testament scholars that Jesus and Peter appear to be using different words for love. Peter using "philia" does not claim to have the "agape" that Jesus asks of him. There is little point in trying to bring out in translation the different senses of these two words, since the whole passage makes it abundantly plain that Peter knows his love for Jesus falls immeasurably short of that which Jesus bears him.

We all live with a sense of guilt, even though we may be assured that God puts our sins "behind his back". We may drag them out (poking behind God's back, as it were) making ourselves miserable with the memory of them. Guilt can be a morbid condition, but not if we deal with it positively, using it as a spur to fresh endeavour in the spiritual life. This is what Jesus enabled Peter to do. The past was past, the sins forgiven, now in the present Peter reaffirms his love, and for the future Jesus gives Peter a commission, "Feed my lambs, my sheep".

A simple commission? Yes, upon the face of it. A privilege? Yes, but what a terrifying responsibility! Already Peter had been designated the "rock" as his name implies, and entrusted with the "Keys of the Kingdom". No past failure on Peter's part had caused Jesus to lose faith in his Servant, for he knew what by God's grace Peter could become. The subsequent career of Peter, especially his courage and conviction at Pentecost showed what God could make of him. God had not finished with him!

Peter was called to loneliness and pain in his devotion to Christ. In the sequel to this passage in St. John's Gospel, Peter is bidden to concern himself not with other people and their careers but the call of "Follow me" at the beginning of Christ's ministry is re-echoed in the last words of Jesus, "<u>You</u>, <u>you</u> follow me!".

The details of the close of Peter's life are scant, but there is a rather lovely legend (unsubstantiated by Biblical evidence) that Peter at a time of persecution in Rome was prevailed upon by his companions to save his life by escaping from the city. As he travelled unwillingly out of the city Jesus met him; Peter asked, "Quo vadis, Domine?" ("Where are you going, Lord?") and received the answer, "To Rome, to die for you". When the vision vanished Peter returned to the city to be crucified, upside down unworthy of his Master.

Jesus still says to us, "Follow me" - as a Church, the Body of Christ. He still says to us individually, "You, you follow me".

We can all echo the words of the little girl, "Please be patient with me; God hasn't finished with me yet".

A45 TRANSFIGURATION

St. Luke 9.vv.28-36

~ Now about eight days after these sayings Jesus took with him Peter, and John and James, and went up on the mountain to pray. And while he was praying, the appearance of his face changed, and his clothes became dazzling white. Suddenly they saw two men, Moses and Elijah talking to him. They appeared in glory and were speaking of his departure, which he was about to accomplish at Jerusalem. Now Peter and his companions were weighed down with sleep; but since they had stayed awake, they saw his glory and the two men who stood with him. Just as they were leaving him, Peter said to Jesus, "Master, it is good for us to be here; let us make three dwellings, one for you, one for Moses, and one for Elijah", not knowing what he said. Whilst he was saying this, a cloud came and overshadowed them; and they were terrified as they entered the cloud. Then from the cloud came a voice that said, "This is

my Son, my chosen; listen to him!". When the voice had spoken Jesus was found alone. And they kept silent and in those days told no one any of the things they had seen. ~

After more than 30 years in the North East of England I am still finding new meanings to the magical word "canny". I think even natives don't understand all its connotations. But I do understand, as we all do, the meaning of "uncanny", i.e. other-worldly, awesome, strange.

Most Bible stories refer to events that are simple and easily grasped, but three New Testament events have the uncanny breaking through of the other-worldly into this world of sense and experience. They are the Baptism of Christ, the Temptations of Christ, and the Transfiguration with the voice and presence of the "Great Beyond". At times of great significance in our Lord's life these events took place, i.e. his acceptance by the Father, his acceptance of the role he was to play and his preparation for his departure. Jesus lived as a human being; but at time of great crisis his divinity shone through in a very special way so that the glory, the power, the presence of God and the splendour of God were made manifest, reassuring him of the care and closeness of God giving him courage and strength for the tasks ahead.

This "theophany" or "showing of God" happened not only to Jesus. We see it in the account of Moses on the mountain (*Exodus 34.vv.29-end*). St Paul refers to both events in *II Corinthians 3.vv.4-end* and the Transfiguration is well attested in the New Testament.

To what extent, one wonders, can this Transfiguration experience be shared by other people? I can testify that I have seen the glory of God in many faces. It may be in the serene and beautiful faces of young people (are not figures of the Madonna and the Saints modelled upon the lovely faces we see around us?). I have seen it in the care-worn and wrinkled faces of the aged who have gained the peace that passes all understanding. In sorrow and in joy, faces may be lit up by that inner sense of God's presence, power, joy, splendour and glory.

A46 <u>ASCENSION</u>   Thursday 2010

St. Luke 24.vv.45-52

~ Then Jesus opened their minds to understand the scriptures, and he said to them, "Thus it is written, that the Messiah is to suffer and to rise from the dead on the third day, and that repentance and forgiveness of sins is to be proclaimed in his name to all nations, beginning from Jerusalem. You are witnesses of these things. And see, I am sending upon you what my Father

promised; so stay here in the city until you have been clothed with power from on high". Then he led them out as far as Bethany, and lifting up his hands, he blessed them. While he was blessing them, he withdrew from them and was carried up into heaven. And they worshipped him, and returned to Jerusalem with great joy, and they were continually in the temple blessing God. ~

Ascension is the most neglected of the Christian festivals. In days gone by school children always had a holiday on Ascension Day and many people attended church. The event that it commemorates is one of great significance; forty days after the Resurrection of Jesus and ten days before the giving of the Holy Spirit, Jesus was taken up into heaven. Those who are sceptical about the exact nature of this event must at least acknowledge that Jesus has returned to the Father from whom he came, for he is ever present and ever living to those who love him.

On the Mount of Olives there is a landmark visible from the Jordan Valley - the slender tower or spire of the Church of the Ascension silhouetted like an upright pencil against the sky, a reminder that this remarkable event took place there. Perhaps the simplest pictorial representation of the event is to be found in York Minster. About half way down the nave if you look up you can clearly see carved in stone upon a boss in the roof the soles of a pair of feet!

St. Luke in his account of the Ascension *(Acts 1.v.10 - 11)* makes mention of two figures asking the Apostles, "Why do you stand gazing up into heaven?". They might well gaze in wonder, awe and longing as their Master parted from them, but they had a mission to fulfil and must descend from the mount of glory to the everyday world. The significance of this event was threefold.

First, it marked a new beginning. As he had promised, Jesus was to be with his followers no longer in the flesh but in the Spirit. This was a curtain raiser to Pentecost and victorious living.

Secondly, it was an end. Christ's victory over death was complete. Jesus said, "I, if I be lifted up, will draw all people to myself" - probably it was to this event that He referred.

Thirdly, it was a sign that Jesus is an ever present friend in our youth and in old age, the timeless One whom we find not spatially but in the heart and mind as we acknowledge him as Saviour and Lord, when we gladly submit and entrust our lives, our dreams, our ambitions and powers to him.

Why stand gazing into the heavens? As a helmsman at sea can gain no help or guidance from looking around him on the open sea, even so we, if we are to

134

gain our destination, must look up to the heavens where our Saviour Christ has gone before.

A47 PENTECOST

St. John 14.vv.18-26

~ Jesus said, "I will not leave you orphaned; I am coming to you. In a little while the world will no longer see me, but you will see me; because I live, you also will live. On that day you will know that I am in my Father, and you in me, and I in you. They who have my commandments and keep them are those who love me; and those who love me will be loved by my Father, and I will love them and reveal myself to them". Judas (not Iscariot) said to him, "Lord, how is it that you will reveal yourself to us, and not to the world?". Jesus answered him, "Those who love me will keep my word, and my Father will love them, and we will come to them and make our home with them. Whoever does not love me does not keep my words; and the word that you hear is not mine, but is from the Father who sent me". ~

It is only in museums nowadays that we see buses and cars with solid tyres. Few living today have experienced the discomfort of riding penny farthing or bone shaker cycles with solid tyres. The only plea one can put in for them is that punctures were unknown - but even then it is only when we have struggled with a car jack in the pouring rain and to find that the spare tyre has also gone flat, that we can think with any degree of favour of solid tyres!

In 1925 we saw the advent of the pneumatic tyre and what a difference this made to our comfort on the road. If we maintain our vehicles carefully, and follow the maker's instructions, punctures are few and far between.

In 1965, shortly before his death, the great theologian Karl Barth was asked his opinion about the state of religion in Britain and Europe. His answer was devastating - he described it as a 'flat tyre Christianity'. Why? It was because he believed the Pneuma had gone out of it. Now Pneuma is the Greek for wind, breath, spirit. It is the word we use of tyres that are blown up but it is also the regular New Testament word for the Spirit of God. This was a very damning indictment of the Christian church, but one we should heed - lest it be true. For some Christians the Holy Spirit is the most unreal and least recognised part of their faith. The use of the term Holy Ghost is not particularly helpful, for Jesus was not referring to a ghost or wraith.

However we speak of the coming of the Holy Spirit, it is our encounter with the Living God, the energising of those who respond to God: it is the imparting of new life to individuals and the drawing together of the Christian community in their mission to the world.

Let us not be like certain "fringe Christians" who look around and see the wickedness of the world, wring their hands and cry, with the old woman in ancient Israel when the Ark was lost in battle, 'Ichabod! Ichabod! (the glory has departed). The gift of God's Spirit has not been withdrawn. Let us look to those areas where we see Christians long separated coming closer together. Let us recognise that the Spirit of God still blows where it wills, and fills his faithful servants with the dynamic for victorious living. On Whit Sunday we ask that we may be filled with the Pneuma of God.

Sometimes the Spirit is referred to as the Comforter. It is true that he comes to us to calm us, reassure us in our pain and sorrow - perhaps he says, "Why so hot and bothered, my child? Lo, I am with you always". But there is another meaning to the word Comforter linked with the word fort, fortitude, the strengthener who gives power, courage, determination.

The Spirit comes to transfigure our lives, to enable us to live victoriously and to die serenely.

A48 HANDS

St. Luke 23.vv.44-56

~ *It was now about noon, and darkness came over the whole land until three in the afternoon, while the sun's light failed; and the curtain of the temple was torn in two. Then Jesus, crying with a loud voice said, "Father, into your hands I commend my spirit". Having said this he breathed his last. When the centurion saw what had taken place, he praised God and said, "Certainly this man was innocent". And when all the crowds who had gathered there for this spectacle saw what had taken place, they returned home, beating their breasts. But all his acquaintances, including the women who had followed him from Galilee, stood at a distance, watching these things.*

Now there was a good and righteous man named Joseph, who, though a member of the council, had not agreed to their plan and action. He came from the Jewish town of Arimathea, and he was waiting expectantly for the kingdom of God. This man went to Pilate and asked for the body of Jesus. Then he took it down, wrapped it in a linen cloth, and laid it in a rock-hewn tomb where no one had ever been laid. It was the day of Preparation, and the Sabbath was beginning. The women who had come with him from Galilee followed, and they saw the tomb and how his body was laid. Then they returned and prepared spices and ointments. On the Sabbath they rested according to the commandment. ~

Perhaps the loveliest of all prayers is that which Jewish children are bidden to say at night as they feel sleep stealing upon them, "Father, into thy hands I commit my spirit" - the last Word of Jesus on the Cross. Whatever may happen to the body, it is the spirit that matters. If the spirit is in God's hands, all is well.

New-born babies have their little fists clenched as a rule, but as they go through life they learn (or should) to open out their little hands in giving and receiving. Some people find difficulties in opening their hands (figuratively speaking) but in death the hands are open.

We speak of open-handed friendship, of joining hands in trust and companionship, the handclasp of true love, the "Peace" that is shared in the Eucharist.

We extend our hands in friendship to those we do not know. In pictures and photographs of Brother Roger of the Taize Community, he is often portrayed as stretching out his hands to the poor, the sick, the outcast.

All too familiar is the outstretched hand of the beggar, but in a sense we are all beggars as we stretch out our hands to receive Holy Communion for we are all dependent on God's grace, in need of his pardon and peace.

Beautiful are the hands toil-worn with loving service. "Thy hands have made me and fashioned me" *(Psalm 119.v.73)* says the Psalmist to God.

A little boy was ashamed of his mother's scarred hands until one day his father told him, "When you were tiny in your cot it caught fire, but Mummy beat out the flames with her bare hands". From then on these scarred hands were for him the most beautiful hands in the world.

Following the example of Jesus and the Old Testament, we practise the "laying on" of hands in blessing and ordaining to service in the Church.

Jesus' hands were healing hands. He touched and people were made whole.

Durer's representation of "praying hands" is ever popular and well-loved, but even more poignant for Christians are the hands of Jesus, wounded for us, "Behold my hands".

137

For true Christians, whether we live or whether we die, there is the conviction that "God's hands are kind hands".

A49 THE VEIL

St. Mark 15.vv.33-39

~ *When it was noon, darkness came over the whole land until three in the afternoon. At three o'clock Jesus cried out with a loud voice, "Eloi, Eloi lema sabachthani?", which means, "My God, My God, why have you forsaken me?". When some of the bystanders heard it, they said, "Listen, he is calling for Elijah". And someone ran, filled a sponge with sour wine, put it on a stick and gave it to him to drink, saying, "Wait, let us see whether Elijah will come to take him down". Then Jesus gave a loud cry and breathed his last. And the curtain of the temple was torn in two, from top to bottom. Now when the centurion, who stood facing him, saw that in this way he breathed his last, he said, "Truly this man was God's Son!".* ~

"The veil of the Temple was rent in twain from the top to the bottom". If St. Mark recorded such an event and St. Matthew included it in his Gospel, it must have been considered a very significant event. The Temple veil was that which shielded the Holy of Holies from the gaze of the people. Only the Chief Priest, and he only, on the great day of Yom Kippur, the Day of Atonement, was permitted to approach the Divine presence through the veil that hid the shekinah or glory of God. It was at the moment of Christ's death upon the Cross that the barrier was removed and the way made open to God. Jesus said "I am the Way and no-one comes to the Father but my me". The tearing of the veil was a sign that the work of Christ had come to its completion.

An intriguing thought is who did the tearing? However high the curtain, if it were torn by human agency, we should naturally expect it to be torn from the bottom to the top, not as St. Mark describes it. Whatever may lie behind the tradition, the symbolism is plain enough - it was an act of the Divine. By his death Jesus removed the barrier between man and God. We cannot tear the veil, "for all our Righteousness is as filthy rags" as the prophet declared, for all have sinned and fallen short of the glory of God.

The Cross opens the way to God; "Him that cometh to me I will in no wise cast out", Jesus said.. Here we see the ultimate demonstration of God's love. We kill God's Son but his love persists. We look at Christ and say "That's what God is like, God loves me like that".

In imagination we listen to the tearing and say "Thanks be to God for his love expressed in Christ". Perhaps in this event there is a foreshadowing of Jesus in his lifting up, drawing all men to himself? What is this magnetism of the Cross?

As a child, not of the mysterious computer age, I was, and still am, fascinated by the power of magnetism to attract and repel. I still don't understand the physics of magnetism, but I understand still less of the spiritual magnetism or drawing power that operates between people. I simply accept that this is one of life's mysteries and realities. We describe people as having a magnetic personality, a facility to draw others to the self.

Sometimes we say, "I can't understand what she sees in him". We acknowledge that in human sexuality the attraction is often irresistible. We may seek to rationalise our judgements, very often with little success, but the magnetism of the Cross of Christ is that which holds mankind spellbound. It is not that a cross is in itself a thing of beauty. We do not make ornaments of a guillotine or electric chair. A pagan, being introduced to Christianity, was shown a crucifix and exclaimed in horror and tears, "There's a man upon it!". Yes, that's the attraction of the Cross - the man upon it.

We are drawn to him because we know that it was out of love for us that he gave his life, an act of supreme grace and of compassion.

A50 TRINITY

St. John 14.vv.8-17 ✓

~ Philip said to Jesus, "Lord, show us the Father, and we will be satisfied". Jesus said to him, "Have I been with you all this time, Philip, and you still do not know me? Whoever has seen me has seen the Father. How can you say, 'Show us the Father?' Do you not believe that I am in the Father and the Father is in me? The words that I say to you I do not speak on my own; but the Father who dwells in me does his works. Believe me that I am in the Father and the Father is in me; but if you do not, then believe me because of the works themselves. Very truly, I tell you, the one who believes in me will also do the works that I do and, in fact, will do greater works than these, because I am going to the Father. I will do whatever you ask in my name, so that the Father may be glorified in the Son. If in my name you ask me for anything, I will do it. If you love me, you will keep my commandments. And I will ask the Father, and he will give you another Advocate, to be with you for ever. This is the Spirit of truth, whom the world cannot receive, because it neither sees him nor knows him. You know him because he abides with you, and he will be in you". ~

Trinity Sunday, so important in the calendar of the older prayer books, is the only Festival Sunday when we consider not an event but a doctrine of the Church (some would say a 'mystery'). Not all congregations are conversant with or deeply interested in speculative theology. I remember seeing once a lovely cartoon depicting a young and earnest minister holding forth in the pulpit to a Church congregation consisting of three elderly ladies seated below him. He was waving his forefinger and saying, "Aha! I think I hear you saying, 'That smacks of Sabellianism or Monarchianism!'".

Trinity Sunday is the day when preachers are thankful that those who are guilty of (accidental) heresy are no longer burned at the stake because attempts at explaining or even preaching on the doctrine of the Trinity are likely to involve the preacher in heresy. Nevertheless, most preachers look carefully at their congregations to see if there is an eminent theologian present before embarking on their sermons.

Colin Morris in his book on preaching on Trinity Sunday suggests the preacher should arrange a strategic bout of flu with a sore throat so that someone else will have to do the preaching!

The doctrine of one God in three persons is a formidable doctrine to grasp. The great Athanasian Creed the Quicunque Vult only "resolves" the problem by making a statement and apparently denying it in the next breath as "The Father is God, the Son is God, the Holy Ghost is God - yet they are not three Gods but one God!".

How can you explain such a doctrine without ending up with three Gods? Muslims are never convinced we believe in one God! I have a certain amount of sympathy with them!

The Jews also have problems. A Jew was knocked down by a car. A Christian priest passing by wished to minister to the injured man. He knelt by him and said, "Tell me my son, are you a Christian? Do you believe in one God in three persons?". The man opened his eyes and said, "A time like this! A time like this! And he asks me mathematical riddles!".

How then do we come to terms with the doctrine? The answer is that this is the way Christians sum up what they believe about <u>life</u>. Life is shaped for the Christian, around three great realities; Grace, Love, Fellowship. All Christians know and love "The Grace of our Lord Jesus Christ, and the love of God and the Fellowship of the Holy Spirit be with us now and for evermore".

The <u>Love of God</u> is where we start and the final reality is the pure unbounded love extending to the whole Creation that God shows to us. God <u>is</u> love and they who dwell in love dwell in God and he in them. Love is eternal and cannot be lost or destroyed. As we look into our lives what matters most is the moment when we experience forgiveness and love. The proof of love is Easter, Resurrection, Pentecost. Robert Southwell said, "Not where I breathe I live, but where I love I live". "What can separate us from the love of God" *(Romans 8.vv.35-38)*?

The Grace of our Lord Jesus Christ : Jesus shows us God loving and forgiving, his gracious words and works. Jesus bridges the gulf for us unworthy as we are and brings us to God. He offers us the promise of eternal life. All this is an act of free love not of our deserving.

The Fellowship of the Holy Spirit : We accept love and grace but what is the impact on our daily life? We are never alone; God is ever present as an inward source of strength to guide and comfort. His Spirit dwells in us, the "love that will not let us go". "Speak to him thou for he hears; And spirit with spirit can meet; closer is he than breathing and nearer than hands and feet".

Christ is the inexhaustible joy of knowing Father, Son and Holy Spirit.

If you are asked to "express the inexpressible" or to "explain the inexplicable", the answer is simply:-

I believe in "the Grace of our Lord Jesus Christ, and the Love of God and the Fellowship of the Holy Spirit".

A51 ALL SAINTS

St. Matthew 5.vv.1-12

~ When Jesus saw the crowds, he went up the mountain; and after he had sat down, his disciples came to him. Then he began to speak, and taught them, saying: "Blessed are the poor in spirit, for theirs is the kingdom of God. Blessed are those who mourn, for they will be comforted. Blessed are those who hunger and thirst for righteousness, for they will be filled. Blessed are the merciful, for they will receive mercy. Blessed are the pure in heart, for they will see God. Blessed are the peacemakers, for they will be called the children of God. Blessed are those who are persecuted for righteousness' sake, for theirs is the kingdom of heaven. Blessed are you when people revile you and persecute you and utter all kinds of evil against you falsely on my account. Rejoice and be glad, for your reward is great in heaven, for in the same way they persecuted the prophets who were before you". ~

The Beatitudes of the Sermon on the Mount describe the hallmarks of the Christian life, reversing many of the generally accepted norms of secular aspirations and behaviour. We hear nothing of the blessedness of those who win the Lottery Jackpot!

We are bidden to give thanks for, to think about and imitate the Saints. But who are the "Saints"? On this point we must be clear in our minds.

First there are "capital letter" Saints - the great men and women of the past, the faithful followers of Jesus Christ. Most of these who lived before the sixteenth century have been canonised by the Church. Their names are familiar - but did they cease with the sixteenth century?

Secondly, there are the unnamed "saints" whom Paul addresses in his letters. New Testament cities often sound beautiful holy places, but really they were, and still are, nothing of the kind. Then, as now, the towns had the usual quota of vice and crime, busy shops and crowded streets, whose citizens were ordinary people going about their ordinary business, sometimes guilty of disgraceful behaviour, open to quarrels and silly heresies - power seekers who often fell away from their high calling in Christ Jesus and yet striving to be loyal in their commitment to him. It is clear that all are called to be "small letter" saints.

Thirdly, there are the modern Saints. Immediately there spring to mind the names of Mother Teresa and other great figures of modern times; but obviously we must not stop there for we must include the humble, simple, lovely souls who are dear to us and who pray for us, who taught us, who care for us - parents, teachers, clergy, and our friends. Indeed, all those common folk who with all their failings believe in Jesus Christ and attempt to follow him in the way that leads to eternal life.

St. Paul said, "We are no better than earthenware pots to contain the treasure of Christ, but he can transform our lives by his indwelling spirit". Let us remember that when God calls someone he does not wait to find someone who is already perfect, "Depart from me, O Lord, for I am a sinful man", said Peter, foremost of the Apostles. Consider too how God bore patiently and forgivingly with his back-sliding "Chosen Race" and how he chose a simple peasant girl to be the mother of his only son.

At the end of a lesson about the Saints, the teacher said to the class, "Who are the Saints?". John, who had been daydreaming and not attending to the lesson, found suddenly that he personally was obliged to answer. Gathering his scattered wits and recalling the stained glass windows in the Church he gave the answer, "The people the light shines through". This gave the teacher pause for thought; it was certainly not the answer he expected, but on reflection he had to agree!

To whatever Christian denomination we belong, Christians subscribe to a belief in the "communion of Saints". Whether we live or whether we die, we are the Lord's. The writer of the Hebrews epistle says, "Since we are compassed about with so great a cloud of witnesses", implying that we are one with the living and the dead. The conviction that we are one with all those dear ones who have gone before us is well illustrated in the following true story:-

A famous nineteenth century cricketer became blind. His son, growing up, became like his father - a first rate cricketer. While at University the lad was selected to play in a very important match. Sadly his father died the day before the match, but the lad insisted on playing, and excelled himself with a splendid century that saved the match. As he returned to the pavilion a friend said, "I'm amazed you could play like that with your father lying dead". The lad replied, "That's just the point, he's always wanted to see me play. This was his first chance".

A52 GROWING OLD

St. Luke 2.vv.25-40

~ Now there was a man in Jerusalem whose name was Simeon: this man was righteous and devout, looking forward to the consolation of Israel, and the Holy Spirit rested on him. It had been revealed to him by the Holy Spirit that he would not see death before he had seen the Lord's Messiah. Guided by the spirit, Simeon came into the temple; and when the parents brought in the child Jesus, to do for him what was customary under the law, Simeon took him in his arms and praised God, saying, "Master, now you are dismissing your servant in peace, according to your word; for my eyes have seen your salvation, which you have prepared in the presence of all peoples, a light for revelation to the Gentiles and for glory to your people Israel. And the Child's father and mother were amazed at what was being said about him. Then Simeon blessed them and said to his mother Mary, "This child is destined for the falling and rising of many in Israel, and to be a sign that will be opposed so that the inner thoughts of many will be revealed - and a sword will pierce your own soul too".

There was also a prophet, Anna the daughter of Phanuel, of the tribe of Asher. She was of a great age, having lived with her husband seven years after her marriage, then as a widow to the age of eighty-four. She never left the temple but worshipped there with fasting and prayer night and day. At that moment she came; and began to praise God and to speak about the child to all who were looking for the redemption of Jerusalem.

When they had finished everything required by the law of the Lord, they returned to Galilee, to their own town of Nazareth. The child grew and became strong, filled with wisdom; and the favour of God was upon him. ~

"Though our outward nature is wasting away, yet we are renewed day by day"

(2 Corinthians 4.v16).

"Let me grow lovely, growing old".

Inevitably all through life our bodily strength fades, but our souls should keep on growing. Ageing is a slope to death physically, but spiritually we should be climbing the hill to God. The years bring us close not to death, but to God. The sufferings of this world are naught in comparison with the glory of the next world. Why then shrink from looking into our inner nature? Perhaps we are not maturing spiritually?

We may be afraid of what we might find inside ourselves! We put up a ring of defences to hide our inner nature from curious eyes and finally succeed in keeping ourselves out too, as strangers to our own soul. A child is unashamedly itself in crying, laughing, free of pretence and frank! An adult, afraid, practises polite dissimulation, defences, disguise and is often condemned to insincerity. Not even we ourselves are allowed to see or suspect the hidden hollowness of horror within us. Professor Joad once said, "Whenever we looked in, we were so terrified that we immediately looked out". We don't like others prying or rummaging around in our personal lives. Let sleeping dogs lie! we say.

We may be afraid of the prospect of getting out of our depth. We feel safe in the shallows, but tend to become more and more worldly. It is safer to discuss the trappings of faith than the spiritual verities. Deep religious faith arises from deep religious experience, but all this comes from God.

How do we give God a chance? We should stop struggling and surrender to God - give up speech for silence, agitation for meditation and trying for trusting.

Anna, the prophetess, had surely learned the secret of growing old gracefully. Her love and religious insights had come to maturity. As she had daily said "Yes" to God, so had she been inwardly renewed. Those who walk with God who are ever mindful of his presence stay inwardly young and possess a spiritual beauty and attractiveness that do not wither. Like Simeon, another member of the "quiet of the land", that is, those undistinguished people who wait upon the Lord, she had gained spiritual insight that enabled her to discern the truth about the one to be king in the hearts of his followers.

Anna through her faith and love was enabled to recognise the nature and reality of the Lord Jesus. This is true spiritual insight. This is what we pray maturity of years may vouchsafe to us also.

We Preach Christ

Reflections on some Gospel passages – Special occasions

B1   ADVENT

St. John 1.vv.1-14

~ In the beginning was the Word, and the Word was with God, and the Word was God. He was in the beginning with God. All things came into being through him, and without him, not one thing came into being. What has come into being in him was life, and the life was the light of all people. The light shines in the darkness, and the darkness did not overcome it.

There was a man sent from God, whose name was John. He came as a witness to testify to the light, so that all might believe through him. He himself was not the light, but he came to testify to the light. The true light, which enlightens everyone was coming into the world.

He was in the world, and the world came into being through him; yet the world did not know him. He came to what was his own, and his own people did not accept him. But to all who received him, who believed in his name, he gave power to become children of God, who were born, not of blood or of the will of the flesh or of the will of man, but of God.

The Word became flesh and lived among us, and we have seen his glory, the glory as of a father's only son, full and grace and truth. ~

"Stir up, O Lord, the wills of your faithful people, that richly bearing the fruit of good works, they may by you be richly rewarded, through Jesus Christ our Lord". Amen

"Amen" is a very "Churchy" word. We don't often hear it used outside the Church, but when we do, it is always in the true sense of the word, "I agree wholeheartedly with what you've said" - "I'll say 'amen' to that".

But have you ever thought out the real implications of saying "amen"? Did you say "amen" to the "stir up" Collect this morning, the Sunday before Advent?

In the Church we are expected to say a "crisp amen" at the end of prayers, but have you really thought out the danger of this? Yes, I mean danger, because today's Collect says, "Stir up, O Lord, the wills of your faithful people", and if you said "amen" to that, you are really saying, "Yes, that is my prayer too", and you identify with all God's people who ask to be stirred up. If then you said "amen", its too late to hang up the sign "Please do not disturb".

148

Do you really want to be stirred up or to be left alone? Some of us often wish to be left alone. Isn't life more comfortable if we are left alone to opt out of our responsibilities? Isn't life all too often a nasty mess of our own or others' making? Don't we often feel, "I've got troubles enough of my own - why become involved?".

Who then is this disturber of our peace? It is "Christ who makes all things new", who says, "Keep watch, be alert". It is the Holy Spirit, the "Comforter", that is, not simply one who calms and brings peace, but one who forcefully stirs up with wind and fire. It is too late, therefore, if you said "amen". "Stir-up Sunday" is not, as some imagine, a reminder to stir the Christmas puddings but a preparation for Advent. Whatever the rest of the world is doing, what are we Christians about? Are we awake, alert, asleep or idle? Are we ready for the coming of Christ into our lives?

Not all members of the Anglican Church know what is meant by the word "Cóllect". They know the meaning of colléct, i.e. to gather. "Cóllect" is a very "Churchy" word. It is a brief prayer used early in Divine Service to express the collected thoughts and ideas associated with the theme of a particular Sunday. The Advent Collect composed by Archbishop Cranmer for the 1549 Prayer Book and based upon a passage in *Romans (ch.13.vv.8-end)* is a masterpiece of spiritual writing. "Almighty God, give us grace that we may cast away the works of darkness and put upon us the armour of light now in the time of this mortal life, in which your son Jesus Christ came to us in great humility; so that on the last day, when he shall come again in his glorious majesty to judge the living and the dead, we may rise to the life immortal; through him who is alive and reigns with you and the Holy Spirit, one God, now and forever".

Not all Christians, and certainly not all non-Christians understand the meaning of "Advent". It simply means "coming", but for Christians it is associated almost exclusively with the coming of Jesus Christ, the Incarnation, the "Word made Flesh", Emmanuel, "God with us", and Advent is the period of four weeks before Christmas when Christians prepare for the coming of Christ into their lives.

When we refer to the coming of Christ, we think of it in three aspects - the past, present, and future, the Christ who came, who comes, who will come again.

Jesus said, "I am the Light of the World". Fifty years ago I spent the night of Christmas Eve in the "Field of the Shepherds". It was a dark night, and in the world around there was darkness and warfare, violence and sin - how like the world into which Jesus was born! Yet there were stars over Bethlehem and

149

light was coming into the world. In humility, as our Collect reminds us, the Son of God came into this world. He came to offer mankind forgiveness, peace, eternal life and to share his glorious risen life. What he asked of mankind in his first coming was welcome, love and commitment to him.

He is the same Christ who comes to us today. "Behold I stand at the door and knock", he said. He comes to us as he came to the fishermen of old and says "Follow me". He comes to us in our prayers, if we will but listen, in our bible reading, in worship, in Holy Communion. He seeks out, and again asks for welcome, love and commitment to him.

He will come again; for we know that we must stand before his judgement throne - not so much to say what we have done (or have not done), as to declare how we have (or have not) responded to his love. Sometimes Christian people over-emphasise the judgmental aspect of Biblical teaching. We need to remember that judgement is now. What we do now in response to his invitation, his call, is of eternal significance, for on this depends the kind of person we become. It is all too easy for preachers to dwell unduly on the separation aspect of judgement (the sheep and goats parable of Jesus, *Matthew 25.vv.31-end*), painting lurid pictures of Hell Fire. A just and compassionate Saviour knows that most of us experience here on earth a great deal of hell of our own making - and perhaps a little bit of heaven. We know that these are realities in our lives, and may be perpetuated into the life to come. As our children in their schools are assessed continuously, but eventually have to face examinations, so there is for all of us a day of reckoning, but the "Examiner" is one who strives to make sure we do not fail the test. "God has not destined you for wrath, but for salvation", said St. Paul.

Again what he asks of us is our love and commitment to him as he offers us his abiding presence, his love, his forgiveness, his peace.

B2 ADVENT JOY

St. John 16.vv.16-22

~ Jesus said, "A little while, and you will no longer see me, and again a little while, and you will see me". Then some of his disciples said to one another, "What does he mean by saying to us, 'A little while, and you will no longer see me, and again a little while, and you will see me', and 'Because I am going to the Father'". They said, "What does he mean by this 'a little while'? We do not know what he is talking about". Jesus knew that they wanted to ask him, so he said to them, "Are you discussing among yourselves what I meant when I said, 'A little while, and you will no longer see me , and again a little while, and you will see me'? Very truly, I tell you, you will weep and mourn, but the

world will rejoice, you will have pain, but your pain will turn into joy. When a woman is in labour, she has pain, because her hour has come. But when her child is born, she no longer remembers the anguish because of the joy of having brought a human being into the world. So you have pain now; but I will see you again, and your hearts will rejoice, and no one will take your joy from you". ~

"The bells of waiting Advent ring", wrote the poet Sir John Betjeman - and Advent is certainly a time of waiting! The secular world prepares for Christmas ever earlier as the years pass, and children caught up in the excitement of the festive season find the waiting well night intolerable - "Christmas is never going to come!".

For Christian people Advent should be a time of preparation, an echo of Maranatha, "Come Lord Jesus", the last words of the Bible. It is an invitation to the Christ who came, who comes, who will come again. If we think the visit is one of our own making, we make a mistake, for Christ himself is the initiator, not we ourselves. He seeks us out, he comes to us, he visits us.

His "visit", however, is not simply a greeting and chat. It is a "visitation", that is, a visit with a very special purpose. He comes in the hope that we will show him welcome and love.

Of course we may be "out" when he calls - too busy to attend to him or perhaps too fearful or complacent. If so, he doesn't leave a visiting card, but he comes and comes again. An encounter with the living Lord is inescapable, however much we may try to avoid it.

We may try to avoid meeting Christ because of a guilty conscience, a sense of impending fate, the "Sword of Damocles" hanging over us - ideas heightened by traditional teaching about the future Judgement; for some there is the prospect of a dark tunnel with no light at the end.

Our Lord assures us that before us there lies the Cross, not only a sign of self-denial but also a sign of God's invincible love for us. This Cross is "magnetic". "I, if I be lifted up, will draw all mankind to myself", said Jesus.

For the Christian the joy of Christmas lies not solely in the festive merrymaking but also in the knowledge that he who comes to us brings us joy.

We can be of good cheer because we know that God tempers justice with mercy and compassion; our Lord has been here before us, he knows our weakness and the temptations that beset us; judgement is not a terrifying hazard of the future - <u>now</u> is the judgement; what we do <u>now</u> is of eternal significance, our love and response or rejection of his love. All he asks for is our love and welcome.

We can be of good cheer because we know that God does not abandon us. He comes to us in the Incarnation and seeks us out. Though individually and corporately we make a mess of life, yet amid the pain there is joy, amid the hurt there is forgiveness, love and healing; in sorrow there is hope; in darkness a light that cannot be quenched.

He comes to bring us eternal life in this world and the next. We may have little or nothing to offer him, but he only asks our welcome and our love.

B3 ADVENT - CURSE

St. Luke 1.vv.67-79

~ Then John's Father Zechariah was filled with the Holy spirit and spoke this prophecy: "Blessed be the Lord God of Israel, for he has looked favourably on his people and redeemed them. He has raised up a mighty saviour for us in the house of his servant David, as he spoke through the mouth of his holy prophets from of old, that we would be saved from our enemies and from the hand of all who hate us. Thus he has shown the mercy promised to our ancestors, and has remembered his holy covenant, the oath that he swore to our ancestor Abraham, to grant us that we, being rescued from the hands of our enemies, might serve him without fear, in holiness and righteousness before him all our days. And you, child, will be called the prophet of the Most High: for you will go before the Lord to prepare his ways, to give knowledge of salvation to his people by the forgiveness of their sins. By the tender mercy of our God, the dawn from on high will break upon us, to give light to those who sit in darkness and in the shadow of death, to guide our feet into the way of peace." ~

Nowadays so many of our friends and family die heavily drugged to relieve terminal pain that we seldom know or hear their last words to those around them; but in years gone by much was made of the "last words" of the dying. Occasionally last words were words of reproach or bitterness, but much more often of repentance, forgiveness, hope, reconciliation, confession, pardon, love. Every Passiontide we rehearse and treasure the "last words" from the Cross.

I wonder, however, how many people know the last word or words of the Old Testament. The little book Malachi ("My messenger") closes the Old

Testament with the word "curse"! "Lest I come and smite the land with a curse"! What a sobering, sombre thought!

Before we answer the question, "Did it happen?", we must ask why the book ends on such a note. The answer is that the prophet Malachi was concerned, as we are, with thoughts of judgement. His people had returned from Exile but the joy and expectancy of their new found freedom had evaporated. Complacency and cynicism were rife, religion was corrupt and stale, the days were spiritually dark, sin abounded, their "robes were soiled" - and yet the hope of a Messiah, a Saviour, the Christ, was still lively in the minds of God's people. But how would the Messiah react to the people to whom he was to come? How would God visit his people - with love or wrath, with blessing or a curse?

Malachi declared that God does not desire his people's hurt. A messenger will be sent to admonish and reform God's people before the "Day of the Lord", his visitation so often predicted in the Old Testament.

Four and a half centuries later the prophecies of Malachi were fulfilled. John the Baptist (a "second Elijah") came to recall God's people to obedience, to purify them as with fire and to prepare them for the coming of the Messiah (the Christ).

Handel in his great Oratorio describes the coming of the Christ and the Good News (Gospel) that broke upon the world as the Word became Flesh, the Son of God came to his world.

As we compare and contrast the conditions of Malachi's days and our own, the similarities become very striking. Despite 2,000 years of Christian witness there is still apathy rife in the world, there is still sin and suffering, there is still the need of a loving Saviour to lift mankind to God. There is still a deep felt longing for pardon and peace, for love and compassion, for the blessings that we do not deserve, but in God's tender mercy and by his free gift of grace we accept, as we accept the Christ child into our lives this Christmas time.

Malachi foretold the possibility that the Lord might visit his people with a curse but the Angels' song was "Behold I bring you glad tidings of great joy which shall be to all people".

153

B4 ADVENT - LIGHT

St. John 9.vv.1-12

~ As Jesus walked along, he saw a man blind from birth. His disciples asked him, "Rabbi, who sinned, this man or his parents, that he was born blind?". Jesus answered, "Neither this man nor his parents sinned; he was born blind so that God's works might be revealed in him. We must work the works of him who sent me while it is day; night is coming when no one can work. As long as I am in the world, I am the light of the world". When he had said this, he spat on the ground and made mud with the saliva and spread the mud on the man's eyes, saying to him, "Go wash in the pool of Siloam" (which means Sent). Then he went and washed and came back able to see. The neighbours and those who had seen him before as a beggar began to ask, "Is this not the man who used to sit and beg?". Some were saying, "It is he". Others were saying, "No, but it is someone like him". He kept saying, "I am the man". But they kept asking him, "Then how were your eyes opened?". He answered, "The man called Jesus made mud, spread it on my eyes, and said to me, 'Go to Siloam and wash'. Then I went and washed and received my sight". They said to him, "Where is he?". He said, "I do not know". ~

"The light shines in the darkness"

Even the deepest darkness cannot extinguish the smallest light; in a lighthouse the darker the night, the brighter the beam!

In the autumn when the nights and mornings become darker we naturally think more about light and darkness, aware of the increased danger on the roads and of a little more "folding of the hands to sleep" instead of rising early.

From the Bible we derive fascinating insights on physical and spiritual light. Everywhere in the Old Testament light is associated with life, growth, health and goodness. Out of chaos and darkness came creation and order. In cloud and fire the Hebrews at the Exodus found their guide and protection. The Psalmist declares, "The Lord is my light and my salvation" and that "Deeds of darkness" are abhorrent to him. In the prophets we read of the "Day of the Lord" being a day of darkness not of light for his sinful people.

In the New Testament we read of Jesus saying, "I am the Light of the World"; the birth of Jesus took place in the dark night, but with the Incarnation the new light of life breaks in, destroying the grip of evil and chaos. The ministry of Christ dispels through his love the powers of darkness, ignorance, opposition and hatred. Truly the darkness of the crucifixion, both physical and spiritual, overwhelmed Jesus at Calvary, but this was the prelude to the light of Easter morn.

In our own lives we are acutely conscious of the spiritual darkness of our own and others' lives. There is much to depress us, unless we have faith in God's loving purposes for all those who love him; only a Christian or one who believes in God's over-ruling providence and love can be an optimist as we contemplate the violence, corruption, dangers, perplexity anxiety, and impurity in our own lives and the world around us. Jesus bids us shine as lights in this "naughty" world, but how can we do this? It is by faith and reflecting the light that stems from Christ that we can do this.

We ask for the light of Christ as we sing, "Lead kindly light amid the encircling gloom", but we need to open our lives and hearts to Jesus who says, "Behold I stand at the door and knock". Holman Hunt in his famous picture depicts Jesus with a lantern in his hand as he knocks for the door to be opened.

"Christ is the Morning Star, who when the night of this world is past brings to his saints the promise of the Light of Life and opens everlasting day".

Baeda in Apocalypsim

B5 CHRISTMAS - Birth of Jesus

St. Luke 2.vv.1-18

~ In those days a decree went out from emperor Augustus that all the world should be registered. This was the first registration and was taken while Quirinius was governor of Syria. All went to their own towns to be registered. Joseph also went from the town of Nazareth in Galilee to Judea, to the city of David called Bethlehem, because he was descended from the house and family of David. He went to be registered with Mary, to whom he was engaged and who was expecting a child. While they were there, the time came for her to deliver her child. And she gave birth to her firstborn son and wrapped him in bands of cloth, and laid him in a manger, because there was no place for them in the inn.

In that region there were shepherds living in the fields, keeping watch over their flock by night. Then an angel of the Lord stood before them and the glory of the Lord shone around them, and they were terrified. But the angel said to them, "Do not be afraid; for see I am bringing you good news of great joy for all the people; to you is born this day in the city of David a Saviour,

155

who is the Messiah, the Lord. This will be a sign for you: you will find a child wrapped in bands of cloth and lying in a manger". And suddenly there was with the angel a multitude of the heavenly host, praising God and saying, "Glory to God in the highest heaven, and on earth peace among those whom he favours!".

When the angels had left them and gone into heaven, the shepherds said to one another, "Let us go now to Bethlehem and see this thing that has taken place, which the Lord has made known to us". So they went with haste and found Mary and Joseph, and the child lying in the manger. When they saw this, they made known what had been told them about this child; and all who heard it were amazed at what the shepherds told them. ~

> Some say that ever 'gainst that season comes
> Wherein our Saviour's birth is celebrated
> The bird of dawning singeth all night long
> And then they say no spirit can walk abroad;
> The nights are wholesome then, no planets strike
> No fairy takes, nor witch hath power to charm,
> So hallowed and so gracious is the time.

An air of quietness, stillness and mystery pervades this night, and modern man with all his noise and restlessness can recapture the wonder of this night. The shepherds said, "Let us now go even to Bethlehem and see this thing which is come to pass". Let us go too in imagination. What shall we see?

There may be distress and hatred around but in the field of the shepherd we can recapture peace and mystery. In Bethlehem the lights shine out all the night on Christmas Eve, and the mainly Christian population welcome in the pilgrims. The house of a friend has 100 rooms they say : "My tent is yours". In his first coming, Jesus came in the Incarnation to find a home in the hearts of mankind. "Prepare we in our hearts a home where such a mighty guest may come".

"Great little one whose all embracing birth lifts earth to heaven stoops heaven to earth". If we enter the great Basilica of the Nativity we are struck by the ornateness of its interior. What a contrast with the bareness and poverty of the original stable. If, however, we wish to see the star on the pavement in the place where by tradition Christ was born, we are obliged to stoop, a salutary reminder that God stooped so low for us. We stoop a little, but God stoops so low in the Incarnation.

156

We are reminded that God of his initiative comes to us. He searches us out because he cares for us and loves us. God does for us what we cannot do for ourselves.

God touches our hearts with tenderness, so that by his grace we become at least a little more patient and loving at Christmas time, more concerned about the welfare of others. Let us not put away this self with the Christmas fairy lights. Let us take to heart the words of the carol, "O hush your noise, ye men of strife and hear the angels sing Glory to God in the highest; peace on earth, goodwill to men." Of course the angels had their priorities right, for peace and goodwill follow from ascribing glory to God.

Peace is not an absence of strife but a creative quality, something we co-operate with God in achieving, human tensions balanced and resolved in love. Goodwill is not a sloppy inertia, but a positive, living, active goodness, arising from sacrificial love like his who comes to us in bread and wine.

B6 CHRISTMAS - Emmanuel

St. Luke 1.vv.18-23

~ Zechariah said to the angel, "How will I know that this is so? For I am an old man, and my wife is getting on in years". The angel replied, "I am Gabriel. I stand in the presence of God, and I have been sent to speak to you and to bring you this good news. But now because you did not believe my words, which will be fulfilled in their time, you will become mute, unable to speak, until the day these things occur". Meanwhile the people were waiting for Zechariah, and wondered at his delay in the sanctuary. When he did come out, he could not speak to them, and they realised that he had seen a vision in the sanctuary. He kept motioning to them and remained unable to speak. When his time of service was ended, he went to his home. ~

One of the tragedies of modern life is homelessness, whether it be the rejected, the abandoned, the dispossessed or war victims who are the sufferers. How many feel estranged, alienated (or in modern jargon "marginalised", or the "bottom of the pile"). A universal cry goes up, "All I want is a place to be!". We cannot separate ourselves from places.

Significant events in life are often recalled by recollection of places. Indeed certain places suddenly and quite unaccountably occur to our minds so that we think, "Now why on earth did I suddenly think of 'Cleeve Hill'?"

157

Often we hear old folk refer to places they remember - places of holidays, marriage, places of singing, crying, places of menace, of reassurance, of hurting or healing.

"Jacob came to a place". This (recorded in *Genesis 28.vv.10-17*) was an absolutely unforgettable experience. Jacob could never forget it, for he not only found a place but a conviction that God is omnipresent. As a fugitive he found that he was even yet in the presence of the God he thought he had left behind in the tent of his father Isaac. He called the place "Bethel", the "House of God", for he knew that this God was "Emmanuel", "God with us".

Jacob "saw the invisible" in his vision of the ladder reaching from earth to heaven and the messages of God and his children passing upon it. This two-way traffic is strikingly depicted on the west front of Bath Abbey where, carved in stone, we see a ladder on which some of the angels are shown apparently falling off the ladder (according to a misinformed brochure) since they are descending (suicidally?) head first - but how otherwise can you depict in "still life" someone descending a ladder?! However, the point is made; there is a two-way traffic from earth to heaven - God is omnipresent, Emmanuel, God with us.

Elisha also saw the invisible, and so did his servant, at Dothan. This was a conviction that there are spiritual forces all around us on our earthly pilgrimage *(2Kings 6.vv15-17)*

Francis Thompson, the poet, laments, "The angels keep their ancient places, Turn but a stone and start a wing. 'Tis ye, 'tis your estrangèd faces that miss the many splendoured thing". We are in the presence of spiritual forces all around us.

The writer to the Hebrews describes Abram's faith; he left his friends and his security. We all have to venture out and leave home. For Abram there was to be a new religion, a new vocation, but God was Emmanuel for him. He went out not knowing where or why - but again with Emmanuel into the unknown.

The Gospels and Acts describe Jesus, the Disciples, Paul and the early Christians leaving home in faith that every place is Bethel, "God's House" and God is Emmanuel, "with us".

The whole Bible and Christian experience witness to the fact that we do not go out alone, for we are encompassed about with a great cloud of witnesses on our pilgrimage.

Often the journey through life is daunting, but take courage as you press on towards the goal of the high calling in Christ Jesus *(Philippians 3.v14)*.

B7 CHRISTMAS - Wise Men

St. Matthew 2.vv.1-12

~ In the time of King Herod, after Jesus was born in Bethlehem of Judea, wise men from the East came to Jerusalem, asking, "Where is the child who has been born king of the Jews? For we observed his star at its rising, and have come to pay him homage". When King Herod heard this, he was frightened, and all Jerusalem with him; and calling together all the chief priests and scribes of the people, he inquired of them where the Messiah was to be born. They told him, "In Bethlehem of Judea; for so it has been written by the prophet: 'And you, Bethlehem, in the land of Judah, are by no means least among the rulers of Judah; for from you shall come a ruler who is to shepherd my people Israel.'" Then Herod secretly called for the wise men and learned from them the exact time when the star had appeared. Then he sent them to Bethlehem, saying, "Go and search diligently for the child; and when you have found him, bring me word so that I may also go and pay him homage". When they had heard the king, they set out; and there, ahead of them, went the star that they had seen at its rising, until it stopped over the place where the child was. When they saw that the star had stopped, they were overwhelmed with joy. On entering the house, they saw the child with Mary his mother; and they knelt down and paid him homage. Then, opening their treasure chests, they offered him gifts of gold, frankincense, and myrrh. And having been warned in a dream not to return to Herod, they left for their own country by another road. ~

A few years ago there was a rash of car stickers in the rear windows of cars. The majority of these were blatantly in bad taste or suggestive of impurity. There is one, however, that appeals to Christian people, one hopes; it runs, "Wise men still seek Jesus".

The so-called wise men of St. Matthew's Gospel were astrologers who held the belief that this is an ordered universe, and a new star appearing signified a special birth.

Whether or not their beliefs were justified, we may without fear of contradiction assert that the Gospel writer was right in at least two of his facts; first, at the time of Jesus' birth there was an air of expectancy in Israel and in many of the surrounding nations. Secondly, the coming of Christ was not an event which would affect only the Jewish nation, but one which would affect the Gentile world too.

What did these first century people expect?

The Jews expected a Messiah, the Anointed One; the later books of the Old Testament abound in references to the "Coming One" who would champion his people's cause, one who would restore Israel's fortunes and bring her back to obedience to her God. Christian people see in Christ (Messiah) the fulfilment of all these prophecies in the "Word made flesh". To those people in Israel gifted with spiritual insight such as Elizabeth, Zechariah, Simeon and Anna (the "Quiet of the Land"), here was the promised Saviour.

Not only the Jews, however, but many Gentiles too shared the Jewish expectations of a Saviour. Writers such as the Roman Sallust, Tacitus and Virgil, especially in his 4th Eclogue, refer to a hoped for Saviour.

Jesus came to a waiting world. "Wise men" are those with a desire for God in their hearts. Are we among them?

At Christmas we celebrate God's present to us of his Son. At Epiphany we celebrate God's love in sending to us, who are Gentiles, Him who is to be a Light to lighten the Gentiles and the Glory of his people Israel. Epiphany is the first festival of the new year. On the threshold of a new year we crave for light on our path. God in his mercy veils from our eyes the things that shall be. We are like a lone oarsman rowing into the dark future; before us the past lies open; beside us we glimpse the banks (the present).

For many there are few grounds for optimism, but for us as Christians there is the conviction that God cares, because we know that God's loving purposes for his children cannot be thwarted, and that Christ is with us in our earthly pilgrimage.

George VI in a New Year message to the nation quoted some lines of Louise Haskins; "I said to the man who stood at the gate of the year, 'Give me a light that I may tread safely into the unknown'. But he said to me, 'Go out into the unknown with your hand in the hand of God. That shall be for you better than a light and safer than a known way'".

B8 CHRISTMAS - The Holy Family

St. Luke 2.vv.41-52

~ *Now every year his parents went to Jerusalem for the festival of the Passover. And when he was twelve years old, they went up as usual for the festival. When the festival was ended and they started to return, the boy Jesus stayed behind in Jerusalem, but his parents did not know it. Assuming that he was in the group of travellers, they went a day's journey. Then they started to look for him among their relatives and friends. When they did not find him, they returned to Jerusalem to search for him. After three days they found him in the temple, sitting among the teachers, listening to them and asking them questions. And all who heard him were amazed at his understanding and his answers. When his parents' saw him they were astonished; and his mother said to him, "Child, why have you treated us like this? Look, your father and I have been searching for you in great anxiety". He said to them, "Why were you searching for me? Did you not know that I must be in my Father's house?". But they did not understand what he said to them. Then he went down with them and came to Nazareth, and was obedient to them. His mother treasured all these things in her heart. And Jesus increased in wisdom and in years, and in divine and human favour. ~*

In recent years we have had numerous examples of children being lost and of hearing their anguished parents pleading for their safe return. For those who think that only bad news is given to us by the media, it is good to know that such appeals result in thousands of people joining in the search for missing children, and great is the joy and relief when the lost are recovered. We can well understand the joy of Mary and Joseph when the child Jesus was found after three days in the Temple.

As the church of Christ we have a natural love and concern for children. We welcome them into the church as part of the family of Christ. Nevertheless we could learn from the Jewish people a good deal about the sanctity and value of family life. From the earliest days little ones in the Jewish home are taught to pray, to obey, honour and respect their parents. If later they rebel (as do most children) at least they know what are the guidelines that they are rejecting, because they have been nurtured in body and spirit in security. If we seek to know why proportionally there are less Jewish people in prison than Gentiles, it may well be that they are more constantly prayed for by their families. When Monica the mother of St. Augustine was concerned about her wayward son, she was reassured by the words, "How can it be that a child so prayed for should be lost?".

The value of an early upbringing in the faith of Christ is seen when we have to "let our children go", for it is then that we realise that in letting go we often find that we "keep" them, or perhaps in time they return to us and to faith in Christ.

The story of the Child in the Temple must have been given to us by Mary, the mother of Jesus, an authentic glimpse of the eighteen "hidden years" of Jesus' early life.

Perhaps so much is made of the search for Jesus, that we tend to forget that in a sense this story is really concerned with Jesus finding himself. For Jesus, this was an opportunity for him (young as he was) to test his vocation, to discover his true identify, to discover his relationship to "Abba", his Father.

Sometimes we fail our children in over-emphasising the family sense of human fatherhood at the expense of the spiritual nature of God as an all-loving Being who loves all his children, for all too often the human fatherhood falls so woefully short of the divine love.

Jesus was never in any doubt about the nature of God's love but for him (as for us all) a "second-hand faith" was of no "earthly use". He had to be sure, and so do we.

B9 LENT - Temptation

St. Luke 4.vv.1-13

~ Jesus, full of the Holy Spirit, returned from the Jordan and was led by the Spirit in the wilderness, where for forty days he was tempted by the devil. He ate nothing at all during those days, and when they were over, he was famished. The devil said to him, "If you are the Son of God, command this stone to become a loaf of bread." Jesus answered him, "It is written, 'One does not live by bread alone'." Then the devil led him up and showed him in an instant all the kingdoms of the world. And the devil said to him, "To you I will give their glory and all this authority; for it has been given over to me, and I give it to anyone I please. If you, then, will worship me, it will all be yours." Jesus answered him, "It is written, 'Worship the Lord your God, and serve only him'." Then the devil took him to Jerusalem, and placed him on the pinnacle of the temple, saying to him, "If you are the Son of God, throw yourself down from here, for it is written, 'He will command his angels concerning you, to protect you', and, 'On their hands they will bear you up, so that you will not dash your foot against a stone'." Jesus answered him, "It is said, 'do not put the Lord your God to the test'." When the devil had finished every test, he departed from him until an opportune time. ~

At the beginning of the season of Lent, where do we stand in imagination? Fifty years ago I stood at the site of Our Lord's Temptations, a most fitting place for self-examination and meditation. Join me there in imagination, and visualise the harshness of the wilderness in that deep cleft of the earth, the blue hills of Moab to the east, to the west the brown Judean heights, the River Jordan winding its way to the Dead Sea, and no sign of human habitation except an ancient Greek monastery clinging precariously to the cliff side.

What an awesome sight both then, and even more so in Jesus' day with the added dangers of brigands and wild beasts. Such is the place where we should stand in imagination at the beginning of Lent.

St. Mark tells us that Jesus was "driven" here by the Holy Spirit. But why, we may ask, and why "driven"?

At the outset of his ministry, the Holy Spirit, which is the Spirit of Truth, provided Jesus with an opportunity to shed the encumbrances of the world, that he might discover for himself God's purpose for his life. But, we may ask, why "drove" - Matthew and Luke soften the word to "led", but "drove" expresses the divine compulsion to seek the will of God. For us, certainly, who are prone to inertia, sheer idleness, lack of will-power, fear, illusion and guilt, discipline is necessary if we are to hear and accept God's invitation to discover his purpose for our lives and the truth that sets us free. Many of us prefer the prison and constriction of our own petty lives to a freedom of life open to the Spirit. If we are to make spiritual progress in Lent, we shall need the Spirit to drive us.

The forty days for Jesus were a time of spiritual soul-searching, subject to the Spirit which "blows where it wills". In addition to a rigid self-disciplining, we should use our wilderness freedom to surrender to the Spirit of God, who loves us infinitely more than we can conceive.

In Lent, denying ourselves some of the pleasures of life may be for many a helpful discipline; but if it becomes an end in itself, it may become a purely negative and barren exercise. Lent is all about positive living, a deepening of our spiritual lives. If we have given up anything, it must surely be that we expend the extra time, effort and talents in a positive way by reading, prayer, meditation and service of others - thus deepening our spiritual lives. Lent, then, is about the freedom gained through exposure to the truth - a revelation of God's presence in our lives and in the world. What, then, of Lenten discipline? The answer is brief and very plain. Let us strip away all the clutter of this life and our own concerns at least for a while, and give ourselves space to listen to the Holy Spirit, and receive the pardon and peace which he gives.

B10 LENT - The Lost

St. Luke 19.vv.1-10

~ Jesus entered Jericho and was passing through it. A man was there named Zacchaeus; he was a chief tax collector and was rich. He was trying to see who Jesus was, but on account of the crowd he could not, because he was short in stature. So he ran ahead and climbed a sycamore tree to see him,

because he was going to pass that way. When Jesus came to the place, he looked up and said to him, "Zacchaeus, hurry and come down; for I must stay at your house today". So he hurried down and was happy to welcome him. All who saw it began to grumble and said, "He has gone to be the guest of one who is a sinner". Zacchaeus stood there and said to the Lord, "Look, half of my possessions, Lord, I will give to the poor; and if I have defrauded anyone of anything, I will pay back four times as much". Then Jesus said to him, "Today salvation has come to this house, because he too is a son of Abraham. For the Son of Man came to seek out and to save the lost". ~

"The Son of Man is come to seek and to save the lost".

Who or what are the lost? Not only St. Augustine, but many others, have referred to the generality of mankind as lost and in need of being found again by God. The phenomenon of dreamers so often experiencing the sense of being lost, of wandering around large cities but not finding their goals attest the well-known psychological experience of insecurity and loss. Those who strive to live Christian lives know that they cannot call themselves "just" persons who need no repentance, but we feel that it is stretching the truth somewhat to call ourselves lost souls. Is there, then, any message in the text for us? Are there lost things in our lives which by God's grace we can recapture? I am convinced that there are.

First, there are lost opportunities. We are all aware of the "if only" syndrome - "If only I had said or done ...; If only I had had the courage to witness, to speak out, was I simply thoughtless, or lazy, perhaps 'slow off the mark' ... was I afraid to appear different ... or was I unwilling to be involved?" Maybe the opportunity has been lost, but the experience remains in the memory and, please God, we may learn from it when a similar occasion arises. God is the God of more than the second chance. We see this in the cases of Peter, Zacchaeus and so many New and Old Testament characters.

Secondly, there are lost ideals. In this world we experience disappointment with circumstances with the world as it is, with colleagues, family and friends, but most of all, if we will but admit it, with ourselves. Jesus was patient with his disciples and with us. Jesus is the only one who can restore our faith in the world and in ourselves.

Thirdly, there are lost enthusiasms. How often we start well, but become bored, frustrated, disillusioned. Then is the time to remember that Christ is the Lord of Power and Might, that with him nothing is impossible. The victor asks us to share in his victory.

Fourthly, there is lost happiness. If ever anyone had problems, it was Christ. If ever anyone had cause for sadness, indeed, for despair, it was Jesus; yet what do we find? We find that right up to the end of his so short life, he continued to speak of his JOY. He promised his joy to his followers, a joy based upon his trust in an ever-loving, ever-caring Father. He came that our joy might be full. He knew that "joy that seekest me through pain". The joy of Christ continually breaks through for those who love him. In this world so many people are seeking to find happiness as an end in itself, unaware that happiness is, or should not be, a goal in itself, but a by-product of loving service. No wonder, then, that Jesus was a happy man!

B11 LENT - Exorcism

St. Matthew 12.vv.43-50

~ *Jesus said, "When the unclean spirit has gone out of a person, it wanders through waterless regions looking for a resting place, but it finds none. Then it says, 'I will return to my house from which I came.' When it comes, it finds it empty, swept, and put in order. Then it goes and brings along seven other spirits more evil than itself, and they enter and live there; and the last state of that person is worse than the first. So will it be also with this evil generation". While he was still speaking to the crowds, his mother and his brothers were standing outside, wanting to speak to him. Someone told him, "Look, your mother and your brothers are standing outside, wanting to speak to you". But to the one who had told him this, Jesus replied, "Who is my mother, and who are my brothers?". And pointing to his disciples, he said, "Here are my mother and my brothers! For whoever does the will of my Father in heaven is my brother and sister and mother".* ~

Nature abhors a vacuum, they say, and so does the life of the spirit. Whether we call this little parable a similitude, a likeness or an allegory, what we are considering is really a parable of "spring cleaning", a splendid parable for the season of Lent. It speaks of an evil spirit being cast out of a man, and later finding his erstwhile home swept and put in order, whereupon he gathers to himself seven spirits more evil than himself and entering again into the man renders his last state worse than the first.

Lent always falls into the season for spring cleaning, for turning things out, for cleaning up. Now Jesus warns that there is a danger here - not of falling off the steps in taking the curtains down or getting the wallpaper wrapped round the head in papering the ceiling, no, something far more subtle! In the seventeenth century Spinoza said that "nature abhors a vacuum". Christians need to be filled with the right kind of spirit. St. Paul said, "Be not drunken with wine, but be filled with the Holy Spirit". A garden cleared of crops in the autumn may be full of weeds in the spring.

The whole point of the parable is that we should not simply get rid of evil thoughts, acts, desires and habits, but replace them with what is good and acceptable in the sight of God. We need to drive out the demon's lust, greed, envy, hatred and slander, replacing them with what is good.

In our Lenten discipline we should be POSITIVE. It is all too easy in Lent to emphasise the negative aspects of giving up and of self denial; of course there is great merit in this, but we should also be positive, by cultivating good habits, pure and wholesome thoughts, desires and deeds. Those who wish to prepare through Lent for a happy Easter should be positive. Having cast out evil, we must foster and nurture that which is good.

B12 EASTER - The Cross

St. Matthew 16.vv.21-27

~ *From that time on, Jesus began to show his disciples that he must go to Jerusalem and undergo great suffering at the hands of the elders and chief priests and scribes, and be killed, and on the third day be raised. And Peter took him aside and began to rebuke him, saying, "God forbid it, Lord! This must never happen to you". But he turned and said to Peter, "Get behind me, Satan! You are a stumbling block to me; for you are setting your mind not on divine things but on human things". Then Jesus told his disciples, "If any want to become my followers, let them deny themselves and take up their cross and follow me. For those who want to save their life will lose it, and those who lose their life for my sake will find it. For what will it profit them if they gain the whole world but forfeit their life? Or what will they give in return for their life? For the Son of Man is to come with his angels in the glory of his Father, and then he will repay everyone for what has been done." ~*

Nowadays we read or hear about awful things which were hidden from generations past because of the lack of easy and swift communication. Some say the "Golden Age" has passed. Not so! Not all is well today, but where and when were the "good old days"? In so-called civilised Rome, blood lust and gladiatorial fights were the order of the day. In early Christian days, the cry, "The Christians to the lions!" was raised all too often. Unspeakable atrocities have been committed in the name of religion in years gone by. Two hundred to one hundred years ago there was often a holiday spirit at public hangings and beheadings. We may take comfort that most of mankind have outgrown such cruel "sports".

166

As a youth, Jesus would have witnessed the sight of bodies hanging upon roadside crosses, as a grim warning to the beholders lest they should also commit a similar offence, for above the head of the victim was nailed a superscription stating the charge on which he was condemned. "Jesus of Nazareth, King of the Jews" I.N.R.I., were read over the head of Jesus crucified.

But what do we make of the cross? First we regard it with awe and then with love as we realise the significance of the sacrifice made for us.

The cross of Christ looms so large in the minds of Christians that we are accustomed to wearing it in public; some find this unfitting, but for committed Christians the symbol of the cross is very dear, and it is unnecessary to point out that before the cross became a thing of beauty, it was a symbol of shame and agony.

Jesus said, "If anyone would come after me, let him deny himself and take up his cross and follow me". To deny oneself does not mean simply to deny oneself a treat - such as giving up sweets in Lent. Provided it does not become an end in itself, that may be meritorious - but something much more radical is involved. It means saying "no" to self, rejecting self and putting God and his kingdom first. It is something positive that we are called upon to do, for the "denial" is a means not an end.

The service of God is perfect freedom in every sense. We are called to his service. As he began his ministry, Jesus declared that the kingdom of God was at hand. In his words, his works and person, God's kingship is manifested. The God who helps and saves mankind has a kingly claim upon us. We do not belong to ourselves. We are bought with a price - and what a price! Jesus bids us turn from self-centred worship to the true and living God. The essence of sin (as with Adam and Eve) is attempting to put ourselves in God's place, putting self not God at the centre of our lives. Jesus calls us from bondage to our finite selves, to the glorious liberty of serving God and our fellows.

This is all well and good, we say, but how do we achieve this? We are not left to our own devices. God gives us his Holy Spirit, the Spirit of Freedom. Where the Spirit is, there is freedom. He sets us free from self, to deny ourselves and to live truly as children of God. This is not a five to six week Lenten exercise but a lifelong endeavour. The time of warfare will be long and hard with successes and reverses until we love the Lord with all our heart, mind and strength and our neighbour as ourselves - but until then we cannot rest content.

Sometimes the cross is trivialised in common speech and equated with the petty frustrations and irritations to which we are all at times subjected. Often such experiences are referred to as a "cross I have to bear!". This is not what Jesus meant by the cross. When Jesus said, "Take up the cross daily and follow me", he is really saying, "At the break of day ask God what he wants us to do, and in the evening ask oneself how far we have succeeded and thank God for his help. What an antidote to the modern malaise of "boredom"! There is so much to do for Christ and to suffer for his sake. Perhaps if we consider the task too daunting, we should pray early in the day,

"Lord, help me to remember that nothing is going to happen to me today which together you and I cannot cope with".

B13 EASTER - Maundy

St. John 13.vv.1-15

~ Now before the festival of the Passover, Jesus knew that his hour had come to depart from this world and go to the Father. Having loved his own who were in the world he loved them to the end. The devil had already put it into the heart of Judas son of Simon Iscariot to betray him. And during supper Jesus, knowing that the Father had given all things into his hands, and that he had come from God and was going to God, got up from the table, took off his outer robe, and tied a towel around himself. Then he poured water into a basin and began to wash the disciples' feet and to wipe them with the towel that was tied around him. He came to Simon Peter, who said to him, "Lord, are you going to wash my feet?" Jesus answered, "You do not know now what I am doing, but later you will understand". Peter said to him, "You will never wash my feet". Jesus answered, "Unless I wash you, you have no share with me". Simon Peter said to him, "Lord, not my feet only but also my hands and my head!". Jesus said to him, "One who has bathed does not need to wash, except for the feet, but is entirely clean. And you are clean, though not all of you". For he knew who was to betray him; for this reason he said, "Not all of you are clean". ~

A Collect of the Church bids us pray that we may "have the same mind that was in Christ Jesus, that sharing his humility we may come to be with him in his glory".

If anyone thinks that humility is an easy virtue to exercise, let him think again! We know the creeping sliminess of Uriah Heap a 'umble man, but there are even more insidious dangers as in the following (told by a Jew). They were preparing for "Yom Kippur", the Day of Atonement. The Rabbi entered the Synagogue, beat his breast and cried, "Lord, I am nothing!". The Cantor came in and did likewise. The cleaner came in and said likewise, whereupon the Rabbi turned to the Cantor and said, "Just look who said he is nothing!" Too much "humility" may be pride!

In the masterpiece of the Old Testament which bears his name, Job the courageous, sincere, God-fearing character has been questioning the wisdom and purposes of God. The Almighty confronts Job and asks who is he to question his Creator so. Job is overwhelmed by contrition and confesses that he the creature cannot presume to understand the mind and purpose of the Creator and repents in dust and ashes.

In the New Testament we find in Philippians the "Kenosis" *(Philippians 2 vv.5-11)* passage which speaks of Jesus divesting himself of the divine attributes, emptying himself of all but love and coming to earth to love and serve mankind.

The Feet Washing at the Last Supper, however, is the crowning example of true humility. St. John omits the account of the institution of Holy Communion (at this point) to emphasise the humility and service of Christ. "Actions speak louder than words" and Jesus takes upon himself the duty of the household slave or servant (or the youngest, if there is no servant) to wash the dust of the road from the feet of the guests.

Apparently none of the twelve felt it consonant with his dignity to perform this menial task. We do not know how the others reacted to the sight of Jesus looking up at them as he washed their feet; but we can readily understand Peter's incredulous cry as his turn came - "You, Lord, washing my feet!" and his initial refusal to submit to the washing - and again his desire to be washed head and hands when Jesus assured him that fellowship with him depended on his acceptance of Jesus' ministry to him.

After Jesus had performed this task, he simply stated, "If I your Lord and Master have washed your feet you should wash one another's feet. For I have given you an example that you should love one another as I have loved you".

The closer we are to God, the closer we come to one another in loving, caring, in tender compassion, bearing one another's burdens. No task is too menial for those who in true humility serve their fellows and the One who first loved us.

If this, as Jesus said, is an example to us, it behoves us as followers:-

To serve lovingly, secretly;
To seek out the physically, mentally, spiritually injured, the soiled, the unloved, the rejected;
To look up at them from below as Jesus did with love, warm hearts and gentle hands.

B14 <u>EASTER - Palm Sunday</u>

St. Matthew 21.vv.1-13

~ When they had come near Jerusalem and had reached Bethphage, at the Mount of Olives, Jesus sent two disciples, saying to them, "Go into the village ahead of you, and immediately you will find a donkey tied, and a colt with her; untie them and bring them to me. If anyone says anything to you, just say this, 'The Lord needs them'. And he will send them immediately." This took place to fulfil what had been spoken through the prophet, saying, "Tell the daughter of Zion, Look, your king is coming to you, humble, and mounted on a donkey, and on a colt, the foal of a donkey." The disciples went and did as Jesus had directed them; they brought the donkey and the colt, and put their cloaks on them, and he sat on them. A very large crowd spread their cloaks on the road, and others cut branches from the trees and spread them on the road. The crowds that went ahead of him and that followed were shouting, "Hosanna to the Son of David! Blessed is the one who comes in the name of the Lord! Hosanna in the highest heaven!" When he entered Jerusalem, the whole city was in turmoil, asking, "Who is this?" The crowds were saying, "This is the prophet Jesus from Nazareth in Galilee". Then Jesus entered the temple and drove out all who were selling and buying in the temple, and he overturned the tables of the money changers and the seats of those who sold doves. He said to them, "It is written, 'My house shall be called a house of prayer'; but you are making it a den of robbers". ~

Perhaps you can remember where you were on some special occasion when news of great importance was announced. Many of my generation can remember very vividly the outbreak and ending of the Second World War. I was in Edinburgh when that war ended, and the whole city went wild with excitement, which is exactly how Jerusalem was described on Palm Sunday. But wait! ... five days later the cry of, "Crucify!. We have no king but Caesar". Why? "What hath My Lord done? What makes this rage and spite? Sometimes they strew his way ... then "Crucify" is all their breath" ... so runs a Passion hymn.

What on earth (not Heaven) has gone wrong? Have we got it right? Let us look again at the Gospel evidence. All the Gospels recount Jesus' walk over Olivet, not by back streets, but publicly accepting the Messianic greetings of the crowds. On the descent of the Mount today there stands a small Church called "Dominus Flevit" (The Lord Wept) from which there is a wonderful view of Jerusalem to remind us that Jesus wept over the city that did not know the things that belonged to its peace. The evidence that in fulfilment of Zechariah's prophecy of the coming of the King riding upon a donkey is preserved in G. K. Chesterton's verse, as the donkey declares, "Fools, for I also had my day, one far fierce hour and sweet, There were shouts about my ears, And palms before my feet". Here was history in the making; a new thing was taking place. There were cosmic implications as in the account of the Creation in Job, "When the morning stars sang together and the sons of God shouted for joy". This was a kind of Re-creation. The joy of the people welcoming their King had to be expressed. "If you can stop the birds singing, hold back the dawn, deflect the stars in their course, then you can quench joy". Bidden to silence his enthusiastic followers, Jesus replied, "If these should hold their peace, the very stones would cry out".

What, then, went wrong? Many reasons can be adduced and probably not one fully accounts for the reversal. It has been suggested that the incident has been exaggerated but clearly the Triumphal Entry was an event prepared for beforehand. Jesus himself gave the instructions, "The Lord hath need of them" (the ass and colt). There was doubtless misunderstanding of the role the coming Messiah would play, for he did not come as a conquering hero prepared to save his people in battle. The Pharisees were scandalised by the behaviour of Jesus and the Sadducees were deeply offended by the Temple Cleansing. Probably out of sheer fickleness some of the crowd were persuaded to change sides. Many, no doubt were apathetic, caught up in the demonstration but their enthusiasm waned later on, as they reflected, "This is not really my scene ... I don't really want to be involved" Probably the nearest we shall ever come to an answer is found in the words of Edmund Burke, the eighteenth century Historian and Philosopher who said, "All that is necessary for the triumph of evil is that good men should do nothing". At the arrest of Jesus the decent kindly folk were not there in sufficient numbers to prevent a miscarriage of justice, but whatever help might have been forthcoming, we sinners need to answer in the affirmative the age- old question, "Were you there when they crucified My Lord?" - for figuratively we certainly were!

171

B15 EASTER - Passion

St. John 19.vv.25-30

~ *Meanwhile, standing near the cross of Jesus were his mother, and his mother's sister, Mary the wife of Clopas, and Mary Magdalene. When Jesus saw his mother and the disciple whom he loved standing beside her, he said to his mother, "Woman, here is your son". Then he said to the disciple, "Here is your mother". And from that hour the disciple took her into his own home. After this, when Jesus knew that all was now finished, he said (in order to fulfil the scripture), "I am thirsty". A jar full of sour wine was standing there. So they put a sponge full of the wine on a branch of hyssop and held it to his mouth. When Jesus had received the wine, he said, "It is finished". Then he bowed his head and gave up his spirit.* ~

One of the most pathetic representations in Christian imagery is the Pieta, a picture of the Blessed Virgin Mary lamenting over the dead body of Christ which she holds on her knees. When Jesus was presented in the Temple on the eighth day of his life, the aged priest Simeon foretold that a sword would pierce her soul, and at the foot of the cross we see the fulfilment of that prophecy.

In churches we often see a picture of a little group at the foot of the cross; or simply the sorrowing mother and a Disciple to whom Jesus commended his mother. In his agony on the cross, Jesus triumphed over suffering, and though the salvation of the world was in the balance, yet Jesus thought of the loneliness and pain of his mother and the beloved Disciple. In commending each to the care of the other, Jesus gives us a haunting memory of his love and concern.

As parents and children we know the close bonds that tie us to our mothers, and the pain and loss of a child. Kipling wrote, "If I were hanged on the highest hill, I know whose love would follow me still. If I were drowned in the deepest sea, I know whose tears would come down to me. If I were damned of body and soul, I know whose prayers would make me whole". Such is the bond of mother and child.

This scene at the cross is something that has endeared many Christians to the words of the Eucharistic prayer that runs, "He opened wide his arms for us on the cross". From this tender scene we can learn so much. First, we can be assured that we do not suffer alone, for we are part of the family for whom Christ died. Even if there is, humanly speaking, no one with us in our pain and suffering, we can be assured that Christ is with us in our agony. Secondly, we know that we do not pray alone, for prayer from the family of the church is ever ascending. Sometimes we feel that we cannot endure the pain and suffering that we see in the world and to which we too are exposed. It is then that we need to remember that God and he alone can, and wills, to look with compassion on the anguish of the world, for he and he alone can bring wholeness to nations and individuals. Sometimes our hearts fail us as we contemplate the future and the burdens we may be called upon to endure. Then is the time to remember our Lord's words, "So do not worry about tomorrow, for tomorrow will bring troubles of its own. Today's trouble is enough for today". No-one is asked to bear tomorrow's burden today.

B16   RESURRECTION - Mary Magdalene

St. John 20.vv.11-18

~ But Mary stood weeping outside the tomb. As she wept, she bent over to look into the tomb; and she saw two angels in white, sitting where the body of Jesus had been lying, one at the head and the other at the feet. They said to her, "Woman, why are you weeping?" She said to them, "They have taken away my Lord, and I do not know where they have laid him". When she had said this, she turned around and saw Jesus standing there, but she did not know that it was Jesus. Jesus said to her, "Woman, why are you weeping? Whom are you looking for?" Supposing him to be the gardener, she said to him, "Sir, if you have carried him away, tell me where you have laid him, and I will take him away". Jesus said to her, "Mary!" she turned and said to him in Hebrew, "Rabbouni!" (which means Teacher). Jesus said to her, "Do not hold on to me, because I have not yet ascended to the Father. But go to my brothers and say to them, "I am ascending to my Father and your Father, to my God and your God". Mary Magdalene went and announced to the disciples, "I have seen the Lord"; and she told them that he had said these things to her. ~

Among the many popular and lovely stories in the New Testament probably none can rival or surpass that of Mary Magdalene's encounter with the Risen Jesus at the tomb on Easter Day. The reason is not hard to discover; for here we have depths of feeling, sensitivity and love between two people such as have few parallels in any literature.

Many attempts have been made to delineate the character and past conduct of Mary, but such surmise is vain for two facts of cardinal importance are clearly stated; first, Mary was one who had an unhappy and sinful background and, secondly, she was devoted to Jesus who had shown her love and forgiveness. Psychologists, amateur and professional, like to make of her a "case study", usually of hysteria, but there should be no mystique surrounding her. She was simply one who loved her "Master", who had witnessed his tragic death, one for whom the bottom had dropped out of her life.

When, therefore, Mary came early on the first day of the week to the tomb and found it empty she felt that her world had fallen apart around her.

The tears of Mary and the pathos and tragedy of her situation evoke the pity of all who read this story. Her love for Jesus is shown in the first place in her coming to perform gratuitous offices upon his body and, secondly, in her (probably impracticable) offer to take away his body for reburial.

Blinded no doubt by her tears she pours out her sorrow to the one she met in the garden until with the one word "Mary" spoken in the well-loved tone and voice assured her that her beloved "Master" stood before her.

The effect upon Mary was "electrifying" and elicited from her the greeting "Rabbouni" which expressed her overwhelming joy, excitement and conviction which we hear again in the joyful words she used when she rejoined the Disciples - "I have seen the Lord!".

For Mary the "night of weeping" had indeed become "the morn of song". "Many waters cannot quench love, neither can the floods drown it". Not to all his earthly followers did the Risen Christ appear, but wherever and whenever there is undying love for him and spiritual insight to perceive his presence, he comes, and coming brings a relationship which transcends all sorrow, suffering and even death itself.

On Easter Day our greetings to one another are (or should be) "The Lord is Risen!", and the reply "He is risen indeed!", instead of the bland "Good Morning".

One cannot help but admire (and envy?) the excitement and drama of the Eastern Orthodox Church as it expresses the joy of Easter in its liturgy, for the Resurrection is not an addition to the Gospel, it is the Gospel. It is the "Good News" of what God has done in Christ Jesus.

B17   RESURRECTION - Thomas

St. John 20.vv.19-29

~ When it was evening on that day, the first day of the week, and the doors of the house where the disciples had met were locked for fear of the Jews, Jesus came and stood among them and said, "Peace be with you". After he had said

174

this, he showed them his hands and his side. Then the disciples rejoiced when they saw the Lord. Jesus said to them again, "Peace be with you. As the Father has sent me, so I send you". When he had said this, he breathed on them and said to them, "Receive the Holy Spirit. If you forgive the sins of any, they are forgiven them; if you retain the sins of any, they are retained". But Thomas (who was called the Twin), one of the twelve, was not with them when Jesus came. So the other disciples told him, "We have seen the Lord". But he said to them, "Unless I see the mark of the nails in his hands, and put my finger in the mark of the nails and my hand in his side, I will not believe". A week later his disciples were again in the house, and Thomas was with them. Although the doors were shut, Jesus came and stood among them and said, "Peace be with you". Then he said to Thomas, "Put your fingers here and see my hands. Reach out your hand and put it in my side. Do not doubt but believe". Thomas answered him, "My Lord and my God!" Jesus said to him, "Have you believed because you have seen me? Blessed are those who have not seen and yet have come to believe". ~

What a pity it is that we sometimes remember people for the wrong or inadequate reasons and their names become associated with their defects and not their virtues. Peter is often remembered for the "crowing of the cock" on his denial of Jesus; Judas's name has become a synonym for a traitor; and Thomas seems ever to be associated with doubt (usually in a bad sense).

Thomas is not simply "Doubting Thomas" but the one who made the greatest affirmation of faith when his eyes were opened and he declared, "My Lord and my God!".

The title of "Doubting Thomas" obscures some of the most wonderful characteristics of the man. He is often alluded to in the Gospels as close and loyal to Jesus. It was Thomas, who, when Jesus determined to go to Bethany where Lazarus had died, urged the other Disciples in the words, "Let us go and die with him (Jesus)." He was brave and loyal. He knew what was probably in store for him and them, but showed great courage. We need to remember that courage is not the same as recklessness. The courageous person realises and weighs up the risk, fights down the fear and makes the decision to face danger. Such was Thomas. On another occasion, when Jesus spoke of his departure (meaning death), Thomas asked Jesus his destination - he had to know; he had to be sure; but he was apparently quite reassured when Jesus said, "I am the Way", for Thomas was prepared to go with Jesus wherever he might go.

Thomas was moreover a fiercely independent man. Like his companions, Thomas fled from the scene on Calvary, but to his detriment stayed apart from the others and was not present when Jesus appeared to the other ten Disciples.

175

It is, however, to his credit that he did not simply accept the evidence for the Resurrection of Jesus while he still harboured doubts.

A second-hand faith would not do for Thomas - he had to be sure - and Jesus, who knew his man, knew also that his doubts must be dispelled. Jesus did not find fault with him. He was concerned for him, for Thomas had work to do for Jesus. So Jesus came to him to convince him and received the amazing tribute, "My Lord and my God!". There was no need for Thomas to touch the body of Jesus; for him "seeing was believing".

Thomas was privileged to see the Risen Christ, but it is a mistake to consider Jesus' beatitude "Blessed are they that have not seen and yet believe" as a rebuke to Thomas.

We can all be grateful to Thomas for his steadfast refusal to accept spiritual truths on insufficient evidence. If we do not know the presence of the Risen Christ in our own lives, it is a matter of supreme indifference whether he rose from the dead. "If Christ did not rise, your faith is vain" said St. Paul and he was right.

In the conviction that he had to do with a Risen Lord, Thomas set out to witness to the gospel and, if the evidence is correct, he may well have travelled to India where the Thomist Church yet honours him.

Some people (the inveterate "doubters"!) may find it difficult or incredible that the Risen Jesus took the trouble to come and reassure Thomas, but they would do well to remember the astounding fact that no-one by searching found the Risen Christ, for he came to them. Saint Augustine said, "I would not even have searched for you, Lord, if you had not first found me".

As he came by the lakeside with his call "Follow me!" so he comes to us all if only we have the spiritual insight to know and respond to him.

B18 RESURRECTION - Emmaus

St. Luke 24.vv.13-35

~ Now on that same day two of them were going to a village called Emmaus, about seven miles from Jerusalem, and talking with each other about all these things that had happened. While they were talking and discussing, Jesus himself came near and went with them, but their eyes were kept from recognising him. And he said to them, "What are you discussing with each other while you walk along?". They stood still, looking sad. Then one of them,

whose name was Cleopas, answered him, "Are you the only stranger in Jerusalem who does not know the things that have taken place there in these days?". He asked them, "What things?". They replied, "The things about Jesus of Nazareth, who was a prophet mighty in deed and word before God and all the people, and how our chief priests and leaders handed him over to be condemned to death and crucified him. But we had hoped that he was the one to redeem Israel. Yes, and besides all this, it is now the third day since these things took place. Moreover, some women of our group astounded us. They were at the tomb early this morning, and when they did not find his body there, they came back and told us that they had indeed seen a vision of angels who said that he was alive. Some of those who were with us went to the tomb and found it just as the women had said; but they did not see him". Then he said to them, "Oh, how foolish you are, and how slow of heart to believe all that the prophets have declared! Was it not necessary that the Messiah should suffer these things and then enter into his glory?" Then beginning with Moses and all the prophets, he interpreted to them the things about himself in all the scriptures.

As they came near the village to which they were going, he walked ahead as if he were going on. But they urged him strongly, saying, "Stay with us, because it is almost evening and the day is now nearly over". So he went in to stay with them. When he was at the table with them, he took bread, blessed and broke it, and gave it to them. Then their eyes were opened, and they recognised him,; and he vanished from their sight. They said to each other, "Were not our hearts burning within us while he was talking to us on the road, while he was opening the scripture to us?". That same hour they got up and returned to Jerusalem; and they found the eleven and their companions gathered together. They were saying, "The Lord has risen indeed, and he has appeared to Simon!". Then they told what had happened on the road, and how he had been made known to them in the breaking of the bread. ~

"Abide with me; fast falls the eventide" is still (and deservedly) one of the most popular hymns that we sing, especially at times of sorrow and stress. It is based upon the plea of the two Disciples at Emmaus who besought their unrecognised companion the Risen Christ, "Abide with us, for the day is far spent".

It has been observed that the story is full of spiritual insights. The two Disciples were walking westward into the sunset, weary, downcast and perplexed as may be our life's journey; but they were warmed and cheered by the presence of their unrecognised companion and ended the day in an excited mood as they returned the seven miles back to Jerusalem to share their good news.

On one occasion Scott of the Antarctic with two of his companions made a dangerous journey over the ice and snow and when they reached their camp confessed to one another that they felt that there had been four of them on the journey. The unseen spiritual presence was very real to Moses who said bluntly to God, "If you will go with us, we will go; but if you will not go with us, we will not go". Jesus said, "I am the Way" and "Behold, I stand at the door and knock". We sing, "O for a closer walk with God". For Christian people the presence of Christ on our earthly pilgrimage is our heart's desire, for the darkest road with Christ is better than a bright road without him. Clement of Alexandria said, "Christ turns all our sunsets into dawns".

In one of the Chapels in the new Anglican Cathedral in Liverpool there is a triptych depicting in one of its panels in modern dress the scene "Abide with us". I find this very fitting, for the theme of "Abide with me" is a timeless plea.

Henry Francis Lyte, the Brixham Vicar who composed the hymn, won the love and respect of the simple fisher folk of his parish. In 1847, suffering from consumption, he conducted worship in his church and after two hours spent in his study presented the hymn we love so much. Two and a half months later he died, but he bequeathed us a spiritual masterpiece. The hymn is not an evening hymn or even a funeral hymn. It is alive with hope and joy, an intensely personal hymn, which speaks of the risen victorious life to which Jesus calls us.

B19 RESURRECTION - Faith

St. Luke 7.vv.36-50

~ One of the Pharisees asked Jesus to eat with him, and he went into the Pharisee's house and took his place at the table. And a woman in the city, who was a sinner, having learned that he was eating in the Pharisee's house, brought an alabaster jar of ointment. She stood behind him at his feet, weeping, and began to bathe his feet with her tears and to dry them with her hair. Then she continued kissing his feet and anointing them with the ointment. Now when the Pharisee who had invited him saw it, he said to himself, "If this man were a prophet, he would have known who and what kind of woman this is who is touching him - that she is a sinner". Jesus spoke up and said to him, "Simon, I have something to say to you". "Teacher", he replied, "Speak". "A certain creditor had two debtors; one owed five hundred denarii, and the other fifty. When they could not pay, he cancelled the debts for both of them. Now which of them will love him more?". Simon answered, "I suppose the one for whom he cancelled the greater debt". And Jesus said to him, "You have judged rightly". Then turning toward the woman, he said to

Simon, "Do you see this woman? I entered your house; you gave me no water for my feet, but she has bathed my feet with her tears and dried them with her hair. You gave me no kiss, but from the time I came in she has not stopped kissing my feet. You did not anoint my head with oil, but she has anointed my feet with ointment. Therefore, I tell you, her sins, which were many, have been forgiven; hence she has shown great love. But the one to whom little is forgiven, loves little". Then he said to her, "Your sins are forgiven". But those who were at the table with him began to say among themselves, "Who is this who even forgives sins?". And he said to the woman, "Your faith has saved you; go in peace". ~

There is an ancient (non biblical) tradition that St. Luke was an artist. This is dubious, but he certainly "painted" in words some lovely and vivid scenes as he recounted stories about Jesus. One of the most unforgettable scenes is his portrayal of the harlot in the house of Simon the Pharisee; the contrast between the abject penitent sinner and the self-righteous uncompassionate host.

Simon's motive in inviting Jesus to his home is a matter of speculation. It is unlikely that he intended a slight on Jesus but he certainly omitted to perform the customary marks of hospitality - the kiss of welcome, the water for the feet and the anointing with incense or attar of roses - all of which, said Jesus, were in a sense performed by the penitent woman in her love. The woman may have been present by chance, for feasts were at least witnessed by members of the public; but maybe she seized this chance to give thanks and express love for a past encounter with the one who forgave her sins. As the feast progressed, her love and tears overflowed and she found herself , a notoriously bad character, forgiven and accepted as she redressed Simon's slight to Jesus by unbinding her hair (a mark of shame) to wipe the tears from Jesus' feet and using a costly ointment to anoint his feet. Overwhelmed with love, she gained forgiveness from the one who could lift her up and grant her pardon.

The little parable of the two debtors contained in this story is a fitting description of the perceptions of the three characters in this story.

Simon saw a notorious sinner, a disreputable creature, one who did not deserve pardon, a woman of the streets. The woman saw herself in similar terms but she was aware also that she was in the presence of one who had the power and the will to forgive and restore her. Jesus saw a censorious unloving Pharisee but also a miserable sinner he loved for her own and God's sake, a life to be transfigured.

"You can't change human nature", we often hear people say and how true this is - but God can and does! Jesus has the power and the will to make bad people good.

B20 RESURRECTION - The Word

St. Luke 4.vv.14-21

~ Then Jesus, filled with the power of the Spirit, returned to Galilee, and a report about him spread through all the surrounding country. He began to teach in their synagogues and was praised by everyone. When he came to Nazareth, where he had been brought up, he went to the synagogue on the Sabbath day, as was his custom. He stood up to read, and the scroll of the prophet Isaiah was given to him. He unrolled the scroll and found the place where it was written: "The Spirit of the Lord is upon me, because he has anointed me to bring good news to the poor. He has sent me to proclaim release to the captives and recovery of sight to the blind, to let the oppressed go free, to proclaim the year of the Lord's favour". And he rolled up the scroll, gave it back to the attendant, and sat down. The eyes of all in the synagogue were fixed on him. Then he began to say to them, "Today this scripture has been fulfilled in your hearing". ~

As a child I often sang the old hymn, "There is a book who runs may read, Which heavenly truth imparts; And all the love its scholars need, Pure eyes and Christian hearts". I was always intrigued by the words "who runs". I had visions of one running along with a Bible in his hand - until, reading it, he tripped and fell on his face! No-one ever explained the meaning of "who runs"; but one day in school assembly a visiting cleric asked the school what it meant. Here, I thought, was my chance to find out, but no-one hazarded any answer - nor did the questioner! I often wondered whether he himself knew. Many years later I resolved the problem to my satisfaction by assuming it meant the "ordinary run" of people, the average reader.

British people were once called "the people of the book" because of their respect for and love of the Bible, the language of which permeates so much of English literature and our daily converse. Unfortunately the widespread neglect of the Bible in recent years has resulted in the majority of young people today knowing little or nothing of this vast treasure house, the Word of the Lord.

Someone in recent years said, "I read my Bible to know what people ought to do, and my newspaper to know what they are doing", but the Bible is far more than a moral guide, its spiritual content has never, nor ever will be, surpassed.

I thank God that in recent years there has been a resurgence of interest in the Bible in home reading, group studies, in Church and preaching.

The Collect for Advent II in Anglican prayer books has always spoken of the inspiration of Holy Writ and of the need to <u>digest</u> the word of God. This may seem a strange idea (though the Prophet Jeremiah was bidden by God to eat a scroll containing God's word so that he might speak out God's word!). The truth is, however, that if we take into ourselves and <u>digest</u> God's word, we become capable of witnessing for God. Someone has said, "We become what we eat", and this is true in a physical and spiritual sense. Christian people are nurtured by the word of God. I cannot remember past sermons any more than I can past meals, but I know that I have been fed good and wholesome doctrine through the years.

Some people despise or reject the Old Testament which was the only "Bible" Jesus knew. This is a great pity because it is in the Old Testament that the New Testament becomes fully intelligible and aids our understanding of them both.

Too much is often made (despite the plethora of guides and commentaries available) of the difficulty of understanding Scripture. I find myself agreeing whole-heartedly with "Mark Twain" (Samuel Clements) who said, "Other people are worried by the Biblical passages they cannot understand; as for me, it's the passages that I <u>do</u> understand that cause me anxiety".

The Bible is the WORD of God. In the Old Testament the "Word" was represented as God's power in Creation and his will revealed to Israel and the world. *Isaiah 55.v.11* reads "So shall my word be that goes out from my mouth; it shall not return to me empty, but it shall accomplish that which I purpose". In the New Testament the "Word" is personified in Jesus Christ, of whom it was said, "Never man spake like this man".

The Bible as the Word of God is powerful to transform lives for it is a book of judgement - "What think ye of Christ?". Someone has said, "Other books I read, this book reads me". Whenever we read Scripture we need to remember that it is we who are judged by God's word. Some modern translators have testified to the effect upon them as they have "wrestled" with the text. J. B. Phillips referred to the electrifying effect it had upon him. The younger son of E. V. Rieu said to his brother, "I wonder what father is making of the New Testament". "I wonder", said the latter, "what the New Testament is making of father".

The Word of God has not lost its ancient power, but academic knowledge without commitment cannot of itself transform the lives of those who read the Bible.

"GIVE ME A DRINK"

St John 4 vv 7 - 26

"A Samaritan woman came to draw water, and Jesus said to her, "Give me a drink". (His disciples had gone to the city to buy food). The Samaritan woman said to him, "How is it that you, a Jew, ask a drink of me, a woman of Samaria?""(Jews do not share things in common with Samaritans.) Jesus answered her, "If you knew the gift of God, and who it is that is saying to you, "Give me a drink", you would have asked him, and he would have given you living water. The woman said to him, "Sir, you have no bucket, and the well is deep. Where do you get that living water? Are you greater than our ancestor Jacob, who gave us the well, and with his sons and his flocks drank from it?" Jesus said to her, "Everyone who drinks of this water will be thirsty again, but those who drink of the water that I will give them will never be thirsty. The water that I will give will become in them a spring of water gushing up to eternal life." The woman said to him, "Give me this water so that I may never be thirsty or have to keep coming here to draw water."

"Give me a drink" is the universal cry of the newly born of man and beast, whether spoken or unspoken, or indicated by tears or signs. Until our death, our bodies "cry out" for the water that assuages our thirst and ensures our continuing bodily existence.

The Old and New Testaments give ample evidence of this God-given boon.
In the Old Testament, 2 Samuel 23 vv 15 - 17 we read of David craving a cup of water from Bethlehem spring which was in the hands of his enemy. Three of his henchmen fought their way out of the city and brought water at the risk of their lives to their beloved leader which he proceeded to pour out onto the ground! How could he drink of "the blood" of his loyal warriors?

The Psalmists spoke often of water as <u>life</u> and <u>joy</u> and <u>salvation</u>.
Psalm 23 v 5, "My cup runneth over"; "Come to the water and drink", Isaiah 55 v 1; "The cup of salvation", Psalm 116 v 13.

"I am thirsty", said Jesus, in his agony on the cross…
… then, "It is finished" he said, and gave up his spirit. (John 19 v 30)

One of the most lovely and graphic representations of "Give me a drink", must surely be the sculpture outside the cathedral in Chester, England, on which one might well meditate.

WaterAid

The picture on the front cover of this book reminds us of our daily physical need for life-giving water, and our need of the "Water of Life" that Jesus refers to in his conversation with the Samaritan woman at the well.

All royalties received from sales of this book will be donated to WaterAid which is the UK's only major charity dedicated exclusively to the sustainable provision of safe domestic water, sanitation and hygiene education to the world's poorest people.

Printed in the United Kingdom
by Lightning Source UK Ltd.
105111UKS00002B/76-108